# Staff Development

## with The Comprehension
## Toolkits

Implementing and Sustaining Comprehension Instruction Across the Curriculum

**Stephanie Harvey** ▪ **Anne Goudvis** ▪ **Angela Butler Schroden**

Afterword by Joanne Durham

*first*hand

HEINEMANN

DEDICATED TO TEACHERS™

*first*hand
An imprint of Heinemann
361 Hanover Street
Portsmouth, NH 03801
www.heinemann.com

Offices and agents throughout the world

"Dedicated to Teachers" is a trademark of Greenwood Publishing Group, Inc.

Interior design and composition: Eclipse Publishing Services
Cover design: Jenny Jensen Greenleaf

The Authors and Publisher would like to thank Henry Whitaker (Memphis, TN), Natesha Gates (Jackson, MS), Diana Sequeira (Tampa, FL), Jennifer Hense (Tampa, FL), and Amy Estrada (Tampa, FL), for generously agreeing to appear in photographs for this book.

Cataloging-in-Publication data for this book is on file with the Library of Congress

ISBN-10: 0-325-02884-2
ISBN-13: 978-0-325-02884-2

Printed in the United States of America on acid-free paper
15   14   13   12   11   ML   1   2   3   4   5

# Contents

# Acknowledgments

Collaboration is at the core of every one of our projects. Our own fourteen year collaboration reminds us that two heads are always better than one. And nine or ten heads are exponentially better than two! So we must thank all of the amazing heads (and hearts) who collaborated on this resource.

*To Angela Butler Schroden*: We can't thank you enough for your amazing contribution to this book. Your voice, your energy, your in-the-trenches spirit make this book come alive. How lucky the teachers in Hillsborough County were to have you working side by side with them and how lucky our readers are to peek into the daily lives of kids, teachers, and coaches in these lively Hillsborough classrooms. We hope this book makes you proud.

*To Glenda Brown*: The leadership that you demonstrate in Hillsborough as the reading coordinator is beyond compare. Working in your district has been an extreme pleasure as well as a tremendous learning experience. Thank you so much for your thoughtful input into this book which we know makes you very proud!

*To Joanne Durham*: We thank you for contributing innovative ideas and thoughtful practices to this book gleaned from the work you do every day in Prince George's County. We have learned so much from working alongside you for all these years!

*To Tina Miller*: What can we say? It is not even a slight exaggeration to say that this book would have never come to fruition without you. We are over-the-top grateful for your talent, diligence, brains, and, above all, sense of humor. We demand a blood oath that you will collaborate with us forever!

*To Heather Anderson*: Once again, working with you was a sheer delight. You are smart, thoughtful, fun, and so attentive to detail that you even noticed that we had not sent in our acknowledgments! Thanks for all you do.

*To Sara Holbrook*: Our favorite renaissance woman. Who would imagine that a slam poet, teacher, and writer of such caliber could also create PhotoShop backgrounds that would make Matisse proud? No Power Pointless here—your PowerPoint presentations blow us away. Thanks so much for working with us.

*To David Stirling*: We continue to be amazed by your incredible photographs and everything else you bring to our projects. Your expertise in technology combined with your easygoing manner makes you a joy to work with.

*To Jean Lawler*: It was great to work with you again, Jean. Thanks for doggedly going through the Toolkits to synthesize the best and most useful information for our PD PowerPoint presentations. We appreciate it and so will teachers and coaches!

*To Charles McQuillen*: Our marketer extraordinaire. . . . We thank you (mostly in advance) for all of the work you will be doing to bring this to the world. Working with you is always a kick in the pants. Thanks!

And to our closest collaborators (most of the time anyway . . .), our families, who never hesitate to chime in with thoughts, questions, and ideas: As always, we thank you from the bottom of our hearts.

The actor Mark Ruffalo is known to have said, "The one great thing about a continuing collaboration is that they know you. And if you're really lucky, they really believe in you." We know all of you and believe in all of you, and because of that, we are proud to share our newest resource with the rest of you.

Stephanie Harvey and Anne Goudvis
Fall 2011

# Introduction

## From Stephanie Harvey and Anne Goudvis

Welcome to *Staff Development with The Comprehension Toolkits*, a companion to *The Primary Comprehension Toolkit* and *The Comprehension Toolkit*. The *Toolkits* are curriculum resources that focus on practices featuring explicit, robust, in-depth comprehension instruction. These practices lay a foundation of thinking so that students internalize ways to comprehend what they read and apply strategies in their own independent reading and learning. *Toolkit* instruction ensures that students read engaging texts at their level, think deeply and expansively about them, interact with others, and acquire knowledge. The book you hold in your hands is written for the dedicated literacy coaches, reading specialists, administrators, trainers, mentor teachers, lead teachers, and others who are using *Toolkits* to help teachers teach students how to think strategically while they read, listen, and view and how to work together effectively. Throughout, we will frequently use the term *coach* to describe these staff developers, but this book is for all district or school-based professionals who work with teachers to implement staff development opportunities with *The Comprehension Toolkits*.

The universe of *Toolkit* resources—this staff development book included—has two overarching purposes: to engage kids in deep thinking for comprehension and to engage teachers in practices that ensure kids' thinking and comprehension.

## Kids' Thinking Matters!

When our students begin to understand that their thinking matters, reading and learning change. The refrain of "What time is recess? When's lunch?" becomes the anthem of "Can we please go read now?" As educators, we take kids' thoughts, ideas, opinions, and learning seriously. We design instruction that engages kids and guides them as they grapple with the information and concepts they encounter every day. We teach the reader, not only the reading, by modeling strategies that support our kids to construct meaning as they read. We continuously watch, listen, keep track of, and document our students' learning, stepping in with additional support as we determine it is needed as well as pulling back and letting kids take the lead when they show us they know how.

The *Toolkits* are founded on a large body of research about reading, learning, and achievement. To become proficient readers, students must:

- Spend large amounts of time reading and thinking in texts they can and want to read.

- Have extensive opportunities to respond to their reading and learning through talking, viewing, writing, and drawing.

- Focus on big ideas, issues, and concepts across disciplines.

- Receive explicit instruction in using strategies as tools for decoding and comprehension.

- View reading as a meaningful activity that is personally fulfilling. (Allington, 2008; Harvey and Goudvis, 2007; Pearson et al. 1992)

## Teaching Practices Matter!

In effective schools, all members of the community work collaboratively. Adults and children alike view themselves as thinkers, learners, and teachers. As members of this community, we strive to create intellectually charged environments that invite deep, diverse, flexible thinking, and we welcome questions, discussions, and debate. Students know it's not merely about finding the one right answer; it's about using their minds to identify issues, gather resources, find and synthesize information, and ask questions that lead to new learning. Teachers understand this, too.

Our philosophy of teaching and learning is expressed in the principles on the facing page, which we try to bring to life every day in our classrooms. These principles are the cornerstone of our vision of active literacy and comprehension instruction. Comprehension teaching and learning are about much more than making connections or asking questions. Teaching kids to think strategically does not occur in isolation. It can't happen in a climate that features fill-in-the-blank worksheets, endless recitations, or the teacher up front with a whip and chair! We lay down a foundation of thinking across the day, the year, and the curriculum in a larger context that includes spaces conducive to learning and collaboration, books aplenty, an atmosphere fostering curiosity and engagement, and a strategic spirit nudging everyone to explore and investigate.

## Principles That Guide Our Work

Teach for Understanding and Engagement

Create an Environment for Active Literacy

Understand That Text Matters

Foster Passion and Curiosity

Share Our Literate Lives

Create a Common Language for Literacy and Learning

Build Instruction Around Real-World Reading

Provide Explicit Instruction with the Gradual Release
of Responsibility Framework

Make Thinking Visible and Audible

Recognize That Reading, Writing, and Art Are Interconnected
and Synergistic

Differentiate Instruction, Paying Special Attention to the Needs
of Developing Readers and English Language Learners

Rely on the Teaching Assessing Loop to Inform Instruction

(See the teacher's guides—*The Primary Toolkit*, pages 16–19, and *The Comprehension Toolkit*, pages 8–12—for a full description of these principles.)

## *Toolkits* Improve Instruction

Teaching with the *Toolkits* implies a paradigm shift from the proverbial "sage on stage" to "guide on the side." Many teachers who begin working with *Toolkits* have already made that shift in their own thinking, and *Toolkits* become vehicles for them to put their understanding into action. For others, more scaffolding is needed. We believe that just as developing the thinking strategies taught through *Toolkits* is critical for students' comprehension, supporting teachers to become more reflective practitioners is the key to using these resources successfully. Just as we make thinking visible for kids, this book attempts to make the thinking that goes into the instructional decisions in the *Toolkits* more visible for teachers, so they can use that thinking as an analytical tool for refining their craft.

Staff development begins with the *Toolkits* themselves. The resources in the *Toolkits* offer a short course in teaching comprehension and active literacy:

- Strategy books develop explicit instructional models of how to teach strategies and engage kids in thinking deeply about texts.
- The teacher's guides provide practical and philosophical background for implementing teaching practices based on the principles of teaching and learning.
- *The Comprehension Toolkit* CD-ROM and *The Primary Comprehension Toolkit* DVD-ROM contain teaching resources and active illustrations (video examples, slideshows) of what these teaching practices look like in action.
- The "Reading, Writing, and Research in Science and Social Studies" PowerPoint on *The Primary Comprehension Toolkit* DVD-ROM and the *Extend & Investigate* book in *The Comprehension Toolkit*, grades 3–6, provide a model of how to apply *Toolkit* comprehension and active literacy strategies not only in the literacy block but also in science and social studies.

To accomplish the goals that we set down in the *Toolkits*, working collaboratively with teammates and coaches to plan, design, and implement instruction is likely to make for more effective teaching than going solo. But going solo works, too. For those people who feel comfortable diving into the *Toolkits* on their own, have at it! On the other hand, we have found that as with all instructional practices, collaboration and collegial conversation enhance adult learning and maximize student learning and achievement. We know that a collaborative learning environment is conducive to communication. That means chairs in a classroom can't be in rows or isolated because it is hard to work with your learning partners if you have to get up out of your seat to talk to them. Likewise, teachers need to be part of a collaborative learning community, sharing their instructional practices, talking about their students, reflecting on their teaching, and creating an educational vision that permeates the school itself. One of the underlying purposes of this staff development book is to nudge teachers to collaborate as they work together to learn more about the "why and what" of *The Comprehension Toolkits*.

Just like the *Toolkits* themselves, this book provides a scaffold for teachers to support them as they implement all of the *Toolkit* practices. We teach with clear purposes in mind, so it is important to unpack these practices to better understand them and recognize the thinking behind them. The big ideas in the *Toolkits* that we will address in this book and that we will support teachers to implement include the following:

- Active literacy
- Comprehension strategy instruction
- Use of strategies as tools for learning
- Nonfiction literacy
- Common language for teaching and learning
- Gradual release of responsibility framework for instruction
- Authentic assessment
- Comprehension across the curriculum

## Staff Development Supports Teaching and Learning

We hope the professional development practices suggested in this book will serve as analytical tools and scaffolds for enhancing all of our teaching craft. Mentoring, coaching, and working collaboratively with teachers are at the heart of this book. Here we begin with what we call "The Golden Rules of Coaching, Mentoring, and Teaching."

### The Golden Rules of Coaching, Mentoring, and Teaching

*Make reflection a way of life*

Reflection—the habit of noticing kids' responses to our instruction and thinking about the impact of our teaching practices—is the underpinning that allows us to continually improve, revamp, and revise our teaching. As we teach, we reflect on the active literacy principles that serve as beacons for our teaching practices as well as our own learning. "Reflection is essential to a fully lived professional life. Among teachers, the finest are those who consider their progress in the classroom, who ponder effective teaching strategies and devise creative classroom activities, who practice reflection to set personal and professional goals and who think on their feet as they teach. These educators are the exemplars and leaders in our schools" (Boreen, Johnson, Naday, and Potts, *Mentoring Beginning Teachers*).

According to Boreen, Johnson, Naday, and Potts in *Mentoring Beginning Teachers*, reflection:

- Helps teachers organize their thoughts and make sense of classroom events.
- Leads to professional forms of inquiry and goal setting.

- Promotes a model of learning that views teaching as an ongoing process of knowledge building.
- Promotes conversation and collaboration with mentors and colleagues.

As professionals who work with teachers every day, we must build in time to reflect with teachers, to discuss instructional practices, to plan for future instruction, to observe children as they learn, to analyze student work, and always to keep the big picture in mind.

*Be a learner first*    Nothing sinks a coach faster than the notion that he or she is an expert. Instructional coaches are learning specialists—literacy specialists, math specialists, science specialists, etc.—not experts. Experts often come off as know-it-alls. No one wants to hear from someone who knows it all, let alone learn from him or her. A specialist is someone who knows a lot and cares a lot about a specialty but is insatiably driven to learn more about it. Passion is contagious. Share your passion for learning with teachers you are working with. This book is filled with wise words and thoughts from coaches and teachers who are learners first and foremost.

*Cultivate relationships*    Relationships matter! Coaching, instructional leadership, mentoring, and any other types of instructional support are all about developing relationships. These relationships cohere around a vision of teaching and learning that is developed through the power of conversation and cemented by time and trust. In the world of school, students are at the center of the universe. For adults to make a real difference in children's lives and their learning, they must be working together, speaking honestly yet supportively to one another, and sharing their learning to create a common vision that best serves kids. Above all, they must trust and care about kids—and trust and care about each other.

## General Overview of This Book

This book begins with a section outlining the basics for getting started with *Toolkit* staff development—planning staff development, introducing the *Toolkits* to your school(s), and following through with staff development to sustain the focus over time—and continues with seven chapters that describe and explore the important ideas and practices from *The Comprehension Toolkits*. These chapters are framed around five coaching structures—workshops, study groups, demonstration teaching, co-teaching, and one-on-one coaching. Our purpose is to support those of you who are charged with helping others to implement the *Toolkits* across the curriculum. Our first suggestion is that you carefully read and review the *Toolkit* Teacher's Guides and the information on *The Comprehension Toolkit* CD-ROM and *The Primary Comprehension Toolkit* DVD-ROM as you prepare to work with teachers around *Toolkit* implementation. The teacher's guides and CD-ROM/DVD-ROM have much to offer in relation to *Toolkit* staff development. The *Staff Development Resources* CD-ROM also provides supporting resources for each of the staff development chapters. Please see Appendix A for the contents of this CD-ROM.

Following are the staff development chapters:

- Comprehension Strategies: What are they, why do we need them, and how do readers use them as they are reading?

- Active Literacy: How do we make learning to read and think engaging, collaborative, and meaningful?

- Text Selection: How do we go about finding high-interest texts that will capture the interest of students as well as provide support for teaching strategies and learning content?

- Gradual Release of Responsibility and Conferring: How can we use a framework for *Toolkit* instruction that scaffolds ways to support our students in using comprehension strategies as tools for learning?

- Modeling: Think-Alouds and Demonstrations: How can we break down the purposes and steps of modeling instruction?

- Assessment and Evaluation: How do we use the *Toolkit* thinksheets and other artifacts of learning to assess learning, guide teaching, and show results?

- Content Literacy Across the Curriculum: What are some ways to ensure that *Toolkit* teaching and thinking extend to understanding science and social studies content?

# Framework for *Toolkit* Implementation: Coaching Structures

Just as teaching our students involves varying structures or groupings, the more effective way to teach adults will most likely manifest itself in a combination of experiences and structures. The most frequently used coaching structures you will encounter in this book involve combinations of the following: study groups, workshops, demonstration lessons, co-teaching, and coaching. Each option serves a specific purpose and will enable you to differentiate staff development based on each teacher's needs. Pick and choose what best fits your staff development goals and purposes in relation to each teacher. This section will provide a brief explanation of each structure and its level of support for teachers.

|  | COACH | TEACHER |
|---|---|---|
| Demonstration Lesson | X | |
| **In classroom** | | |
| Co-Teaching | | X |
| Coaching | | X |
| **Out of classroom** | | |
| Workshop | X | |
| Study Group | X | |

*Workshops*  Workshops—organized and run by a coach based on the needs of teachers—provide time for teachers to learn, discuss, and collaborate with colleagues about the essential elements needed to be successful educators. The workshop model—whether weekly, biweekly, or monthly—occurs over time and provides necessary information to understand the "why behind the what." Workshops offer the perfect structure to share information that is new to teachers, allowing all participants to hear a consistent message and reflect on it. Workshops open up teachers' thinking as they learn about *Toolkit* practices and plans for instruction. When combined with follow-up coaching, workshops offer a powerful and supportive professional development structure.

*Study groups*    Study groups allow the coach and teachers to collectively study a professional text, topic, or classroom challenge. These are similar to the workshops we provide, except that in study groups the coach, trainer, or mentor serves as facilitator rather than presenter. In addition to discussing and studying specific topics, study groups allow time for participants to truly collaborate as teachers review *Toolkit* components, read professional articles, assess authentic student work samples, evaluate data, plan instruction, and so on. The study group option is flexible and may take several meetings to explore a concept or could even last an entire year for an in-depth study of a topic. Most of the study groups in this book focus on the core of the *Toolkits*, including delving into the *Toolkit* Teacher's Guides, looking closely at the strategy books, and investigating other topics that emerge in relation to *Toolkit* instruction and active literacy.

*Demonstration lessons*    Demonstration lessons by definition are just that, demonstrations by the staff developer of the teaching moves and teaching language of the lesson. Demonstration lessons will support teachers as they get started with the *Toolkits*, giving them a clear idea of what *Toolkit* instruction looks and sounds like with real kids in real classrooms. Although you can demonstrate *Toolkit* lessons for individual teachers, demonstration lessons are most effective when grade-level teams or small groups of teachers observe the lesson while taking notes and jotting down thoughts and questions. Since the observing teachers typically sit in a group watching the coach deliver the lesson, this type of coaching structure is often referred to as a *fishbowl*. These fishbowl lessons allow for rich in-depth discussions about how teaching moves and teaching language foster engagement and learning. We follow a three-step framework when conducting these demonstrations:

1. **Prebrief.** The coach starts by unpacking the lesson goals and purposes, sharing the teaching language and teaching moves of the lesson, explaining the reasons for text selection, and determining expectations for student performance. The prebrief also offers opportunities for troubleshooting possible lesson pitfalls.

2. **Demonstration lesson.** The coach teaches the lesson while teachers observe, scribe teaching moves and teaching language, record observations and notes, and gather student work to be analyzed and discussed following the lesson.

3. **Debrief.** Participants reflect on the purpose, goals, teaching moves and teaching language, and student engagement as well as

the impact the lesson had on student learning. Questions to consider include: *What learning was expected? How did the teaching moves and teaching language support student learning? What did you notice about student engagement? What did you notice about student learning? Based on student outcomes and lesson goals, where would you go next with the lesson?*

This three-step framework elicits rich conversation around pedagogy, beliefs, and expectations. Demonstration lessons are a powerful coaching structure and provide both opportunities for colleague conversations about teaching and learning and support for teachers to go back and try the lesson on their own. Demonstration lessons can be the catalyst that encourages teachers to take the next step and take advantage of individualized coaching opportunities.

*Co-Teaching*    Co-teaching is a carefully scaffolded teaching experience, guided by the coach, that fully engages the classroom teacher in teaching the lesson alongside the coach. For effective co-teaching, the coach and teacher must engage in a well-thought-out planning session beforehand in order to coordinate tasks and responsibilities throughout the lesson. The success of co-teaching also depends on knowing students well and adapting the lessons to students' learning needs and interests. The classroom teacher is generally the most important resource here as he or she knows the students better than anyone. Following are some considerations as you plan a co-teaching lesson with your colleague:

- Discuss and think about students as readers and learners. Explore what they are currently studying, what reading looks like in the classroom, what is working and what is not, and what the special needs of individual students are, and ascertain the rituals and routines that are currently in place.

- Read through the lesson together (coach and teacher), deciding how to share teaching moves and teaching language. Consider lesson focus, student expectations, big ideas in the topic, choice of text, and the best way to break up the lesson according to the gradual release of responsibility model.

- Co-teach the lesson, paying attention to each other as well as to the students' reading and learning behaviors. If there are teacher observers in the room, encourage them to scribe the teaching moves and language and to jot down their questions and thoughts.

▪ Reflect both on student reading and learning and on the lesson outcomes after the lesson. If there were teacher observers, have them turn and talk to each other to process what they observed. Plan for subsequent instruction based on assessing the students' oral and written responses. Discuss which students might need additional instruction or which students might be ready to work independently, and define next steps.

*Coaching*   Coaching is a one-on-one in-class opportunity for a coach to demonstrate or observe a lesson and provide on-the-spot help. The coaching focus is decided by the teacher and might include using essential teaching language, looking at the amount of teacher talk versus student talk, or paying close attention to student engagement. The most effective coaching sessions include (1) a pre-conference or prebrief, (2) a lesson, and (3) a post-conference or debrief. First, the coach and the teacher have a pre-lesson conference to establish the coaching focus. Then either the coach or the teacher teaches the lesson while the other observes and takes notes. Following the lesson, both the coach and the teacher discuss the lesson based on the coaching focus. The end of one coaching session often leads to the beginning of the next as a new "aha moment" or revelation is discovered. Coaching is the most supportive structure on the continuum as it is based on a one-on-one relationship between the teacher and the coach and is tailored to the specific needs of each individual teacher.

## Introducing Angela Butler—Our Co-Author and Staff Developer Extraordinaire!

Now we have the great pleasure of introducing Angela Butler, Hillsborough County (Florida) district reading specialist, coach, passionate learner, and contributing author of this book. We met Angela as she and Glenda Brown, Hillsborough County elementary reading supervisor, began a district-wide implementation of *The Comprehension Toolkits*. How lucky we were that Angela and Glenda were at the helm as Hillsborough rolled out the *Toolkit*! They are a smart, thoughtful, pragmatic, and delightful pair of educators who recognized early on the possibilities that *Toolkit* implementation and application could bring to the kids of Hillsborough County. So this book, in addition to supporting strong professional development centered on the *Toolkits*, will give you an insider's view of how one group of educators supported teachers across a large district to implement *Toolkit* comprehension instruction and active literacy.

As you read, you will hear straight talk from Angela, who has been on the ground and in the trenches in her district for over a dozen years, supporting teachers across the district to implement all-around best practices as they use the *Toolkits*. Each chapter begins with a vignette from Angela depicting a situation she experienced as a coach working with teachers to implement *Toolkit* comprehension instruction in her district. The body of each chapter includes a variety of coaching structures—workshops, study groups, demonstration lessons, and one-on-one coaching—that Angela uses to support teachers as they implement and sustain their efforts with *Toolkit* instruction. So take it away, Angela!

**Hi there, Angela here.** So I will begin at the beginning! Over a dozen years ago, the elementary reading department of my very large school district (the eighth largest in the nation with 142 elementary schools) decided to train a cadre of elementary teachers to become reading coaches. The role was new, unfamiliar, and hard to define, but as a passionate lover of literacy teaching and learning, I knew that teachers mattered a lot! And I knew that teaching truly is "rocket science"! I believed wholeheartedly that teachers deserved support to do the amazing work they do with kids every day, so I joined the group to learn more about what I could do to support teachers as they engaged in literacy teaching and learning.

My first coaching assignment was at two elementary schools in our district. It wasn't easy. I was enthusiastic and energetic for sure, but I was also young and inexperienced, working in some cases with veteran teachers with many more teaching years under their belts than I had. Some welcomed me with open arms, others looked askance, and some clearly distrusted me. There were nights I could barely see the road through my tears as I drove home. But I didn't give up. I continued to believe that teaching is a collaborative venture and that all teachers deserve support, not because they are lacking talent or ability but because teaching is very hard work, and working and learning together offered the best opportunity for success.

I spent most of that first year soliciting business—volunteering to come in and "try something out" or assist with assessments. Slowly but surely, a few teachers began to engage with me. During the first quarter of the second year, a stellar second grade teacher, Mrs. Wheeler, asked me to come in and coach her on her shared reading lesson. It was a glorious day!

I don't remember the book she used or her teaching point, but I will never forget the conversation we had following the lesson. It was spirited, engaging, and thought-provoking. Our professional relationship remained a constant throughout my time at Springhead Elementary School, and it taught me that effective coaching is all about relationships, developed through the power of conversation and collaboration, cemented with time and trust.

I worked as a school-based coach for four years, veered off into school administration for a time, and now work as a district resource teacher, essentially a reading coach at the district level. In that role, I work with numerous schools of all shapes and sizes—schools with high SES and low SES, schools with enrollments of as few as 300 students and schools with more than 1,000 students. I write and provide district-wide literacy professional development, including the staff development continuum we use to implement *The Primary Comprehension Toolkit* and *The Comprehension Toolkit* across our district. I work with teachers, reading specialists, and principals, observing in classrooms, modeling instruction, coaching teachers, and facilitating conversations about best literacy practices. I absolutely love my job!

As I compare that first day on the job at Springhead Elementary, when I wasn't even able to define my role, to today, when I am still coaching a dozen years later, I can say without hesitation that the role of a coach has two main attributes:

- **Ever- changing.** No two days are ever alike. Embrace the randomness! Even though you might begin with one common goal (for example, developing thinking strategies through *The Comprehension Toolkit*), your role will change depending on the needs of teachers. You will quickly see that some teachers dive right in while other teachers stick the proverbial toe in the shallow end, and still others may even reject your support entirely. It is your role to continue to believe everyone will join in eventually. While that may or may not ever happen, hoping and acting as if they will become a part of your collegial community of educators increases the chances they will come to value the common goal and your coaching support. Embracing the randomness takes coaching from frustrating to invigorating.

- **Agenda free.** Coaching is agenda free . . . kind of. As a literacy coach, one of your primary responsibilities is to drop **your** agenda at the classroom door and pick up the **teacher's** agenda when you cross the threshold. Dropping your agenda honors the risk taken by the teacher to invite you in and establishes trust in the relationship. But this is not always so easy. The teacher may suggest a coaching focus, but as you watch the lesson unfold, you notice something else. The lesson ends, and you have a decision to make: Are you going to address what you noticed or what the teacher asked for? Being agenda free means you are going to honor her agenda. It's not about you; it's about the teacher and ultimately about the students, and that's where the "agenda free . . . kind of" comes in. You will embrace the teacher's agenda but never abandon the agenda of **all** students to get the best possible education. So as you build trust, you will reflect on the teacher's focus first but inch in with what you noticed as well.

Coaching is a multifaceted operation, frequently challenging, sometimes frustrating, but always rewarding. How lucky we are to work so intimately with teachers as they work so closely with kids! Because in the end, as we all know, it is all about the teacher!

*The Comprehension Toolkit* was a natural fit for our district as it was based on our district's beliefs about literacy: the gradual release of responsibility, instruction built around real-world reading, collaborative learning and thinking, and the importance of understanding texts. Finding a resource that matched our beliefs was rare enough, but finding a resource that matched our beliefs **and** increased student achievement through increased teacher effectiveness was like hitting the lottery!

From the 2006–2007 school year when the district purchased *The Comprehension Toolkit* for every third to fifth grade classroom until the present, the percentage of students in grades 3–5 scoring proficient on the Florida Comprehensive Assessment Test (FCAT) in reading has consistently remained between 68 and 71 percent. This is significant because at certain grade levels, this was an increase of 14 percentage points from years 2001–2006 (before the *Toolkit* was purchased), when the percentage of students in grades 3–5 scoring proficient ranged from a low of 54 percent to a high of 68 percent. Additionally, the percentage of students scoring at the highest level of achievement (level 5) in grades 3–5 has increased each year between 2006 and 2010.

From a school-level perspective, I will point to the 2006–2007 school year at one elementary school where I spent the **entire** year working with the administration and grade 3–5 teachers to implement *The Comprehen-*

*sion Toolkit* in the ways we demonstrate in this book. Based on the FCAT, learning gain scores in reading increased 10 percentile points from the previous school year. Students in the bottom quartile increased 21 percentile points in reading. *The Comprehension Toolkit* increases student achievement because it increases teacher effectiveness and student engagement.

Third grade teacher Heather Smith sums it up best: "I really didn't know how to teach comprehension. I've known for years that many of my third grade kids could read the words but often didn't understand what they read, but I had no idea what to do about it. Now I have the *Toolkit*, and I know what to do and how to do it. *The Comprehension Toolkit* has taught teachers how to teach comprehension, and our kids are reading, thinking, and understanding better than ever."

■

So there you have it. Supporting teachers to implement *The Comprehension Toolkits* over time has made a big difference for kids in Angela's district as well as in many other districts we know. But if the *Toolkits*, with all of their moving parts, seem overwhelming, working collaboratively to learn about, unpack, and understand the thinking behind *Toolkit* comprehension instruction and active literacy can be a huge help as you move toward a full implementation of *Toolkit* practices across the curriculum.

In conclusion, we would like to quote from Peter Johnston's foreword in *Responsive Literacy Coaching* by Cheryl Dozier (Stenhouse 2006). Johnston sums it up best when he says:

> Teaching doesn't improve by force. It improves as teachers come to understand what they are doing, why they are doing [it], and with whom they are doing it. They need to know what their options are, and need a community of colleagues who support their problem-solving and encourage them to challenge themselves. Responsive coaching helps teachers capitalize on their own literacy and learning experiences without becoming trapped in them. It creates social spaces in which teachers can feel safe sharing half-baked possibilities, analyzing errors, and seeking and examining evidence while keeping their heads and their eyes on the big picture—educating children for an advanced and rapidly changing democracy.

We believe that teaching kids to think strategically, interact with each other, respond to texts, and question, analyze, and synthesize what they hear, read, and view will lead to citizens who can contribute and make a difference in the twenty-first century. We also believe that supporting teachers to help learners do this is our most important responsibility as we look to the future. We hope that *Staff Development with The Comprehension Toolkits* will serve as a valuable tool as you implement the *Toolkits* with teachers and kids in your schools and districts.

**I (Angela) was meeting with** a team of kindergarten teachers who were new to the *Toolkit*. Their principal believed in the *Toolkit* and expected it to be used with the students. The teachers were just starting to implement *Toolkit* comprehension instruction. I wanted to discover their honest feelings about teaching with the *Toolkit*, so I began my demonstration lesson prebrief by saying, "Tell me a little bit about how the *Toolkit* is working for you."

After they had looked at each other for a few moments, the teacher in whose classroom I would soon be modeling turned to me and said, "I'll admit it. I haven't really used it much at all."

Encouraged by her honesty, I continued my questioning: "Have you not had the time, or is it something else?"

She hesitated a moment and said, "Well, my kids don't seem to think much. I mean, they're only kindergartners."

Taken aback, I asked, "They don't think during reading or ever?"

She shook her head and replied, "Mostly during reading. They think on the playground." She smiled.

We all laughed, and I briefly explained that the first strategy book in both the primary and the intermediate *Toolkits* focuses specifically on teaching children to monitor their comprehension—in other words, to be aware of the thinking they do when they read, listen, or view. After reviewing the teaching moves and lesson goals, I reminded the teachers that while I wanted them to notice my teaching language and moves, I wanted them to spend most of their time noticing student thinking and learning.

As you might expect, it can be a bit overwhelming to read an engaging text to a class full of spirited kindergartners and then ask them to think about what they'd heard, to talk to each other about their thinking, and to sketch or write their thoughts. But the kids did not disappoint. They were awesome! During our debriefing session, even before I had a chance to say anything, the classroom teacher looked at me and said, "Oh my gosh! I honestly didn't know they could do that—and I especially didn't know Zach could do that." The rest of our conversation revolved around additional comprehension strategies in the *Toolkit* and how teachers might be able to work *Toolkit* instruction into their week, acknowledging that some of the lessons might need to be broken up over two days. We all left the learning session knowing that students, even five- and six-year-olds, **think** when they read, listen, or view and that the *Toolkit* could facilitate that thinking.

# *Toolkits* and Staff Development: What, Why, and When

Hours of classroom observation and conversations with teachers reveal that comprehension strategies and the teaching methods that ensure deep comprehension are not always completely familiar to teachers. Many of our conversations begin with the same statement: "My kids can read, but they don't understand what they are reading." With good intentions, these teachers redouble their efforts, primarily teaching the standards tested on state assessments, but they seldom have the impact they hope for. Even their basal reading series revolves mainly around state-tested skills. Students are often asked to answer a question but are rarely shown how to understand. Strategies such as making connections or drawing conclusions are mentioned but are not explicitly taught. Where do we go from here?

Enter *The Comprehension Toolkits*. The two *Toolkit* packages—*The Primary Comprehension Toolkit* for grades K–2 and *The Comprehension Toolkit* for grades 3–6—both offer models of explicit instruction in research-based comprehension strategies: monitoring comprehension, activating and connecting prior knowledge to new information, asking questions, inferring and visualizing, determining importance, and summarizing and synthesizing. Moreover, this instruction focuses on high-interest *nonfiction* texts, a perfect vehicle for facilitating the transfer of informational thinking and learning to content-area studies. By working through the strategy books and other *Toolkit* components appropriate to their grade and tailoring the teaching model to their own curriculum topics, resources, and text selections, teachers can promote the kinds of expansive thinking we are looking for.

But teaching comprehension goes beyond direct instruction in a handful of strategies. As critical as these strategies are, it is the teacher who makes all the difference: the learning environment she establishes, the texts she chooses, the teaching methods she uses to engage and support students as they make sense of texts. It is this dimension of teaching comprehension that most cries out for intensive staff development, and the *Toolkits* provide a model for employing effective methods for teaching not only comprehension but any subject area. The *Toolkit* packages provide strong support for opening up the classroom to active literacy practices. The strategy lessons themselves model myriad ways to engage and prompt students to construct their own meaning. The teacher's guides describe and provide the rationales for fundamental teaching practices. *The Comprehension Toolkit* CD-ROM and *The Primary Comprehension Toolkit* DVD-ROM provide photographic and video models of what a classroom and a lesson look and sound like. *The Primary Toolkit* Teacher's Guide and the *Extend & Investigate* book in *The Comprehension Toolkit* for grades 3–6 show how to take comprehension across the curriculum in science and social studies.

There you have it, a solution to a two-pronged problem: (1) students needing to learn how to comprehend deeply and (2) teachers needing to learn how to teach deep comprehension. The *Toolkits* focus on the idea of deep comprehension instruction for students, but they don't ignore the need for teacher support. They don't just mention strategies; they provide explicit ways to teach kids how to be strategic, thoughtful readers. The lessons include the teacher language and teacher moves that are vitally important for teachers who hesitate to dive in and teach comprehension this way. Even if explicit comprehension instruction in an active literacy setting represents a paradigm shift for many teachers, the *Toolkits* help them make that shift.

At the same time, it's clear that if the goal is to open up classrooms to effective literacy practices, more than a multimedia kit is necessary. The *Toolkits* provide the springboard, but teachers also need support to understand *Toolkit* practices and to implement them in the day-to-day teaching of comprehension strategies. While the *Toolkits* offer a scaffold for good teaching, they will be even more effective if (1) they promote ongoing collaborative work around comprehension, and (2) they are implemented through a sustained district- or school-wide dedication to comprehension instruction and powerful literacy practices. The series of coaching sessions in this book, beginning with a general orientation to the *Toolkits* and extending into the school year with ongoing workshops and in-school sessions, is designed to support just such an effort.

## Planning for *Toolkit* Staff Development

When implementing the *Toolkits*, it is smart to have a plan for introducing the materials to teachers and for following through with staff development. The best place to begin is by studying the *Toolkits* yourself in depth. Begin with the teacher's guides, *The Comprehension Toolkit* CD-ROM, and *The Primary Comprehension Toolkit* DVD-ROM. These components will give you the information you need to discover what is in the *Toolkits* and where to find it. For instance, there are extensive bibliographies of children's books, magazines, websites, and professional books in *Keep Reading! A Source Book of Short Text* in the primary *Toolkit* and the *Extend & Investigate* book in the intermediate *Toolkit*. These are the kinds of resources that can get lost in the shuffle. So before you start with teachers, get up-close and personal with your *Toolkits*. Take some time to familiarize yourself with all of the resources that the *Toolkits* offer both teachers and kids alike.

Establishing a common focus with all stakeholders, administrators, teacher leaders, coaches, and teachers is critical to successful *Toolkit* implementation and sustainability. Sharing a common focus allows deep conversations and learning to occur among all teachers involved with student learning. Having a common focus provides a goal that all teaching and learning decisions will be designed to reach.

### Time and Other Resources

Whether scheduling coaching sessions is your responsibility or someone else's, you'll want to advocate for the time and material support to make your *Toolkit* staff development maximally effective. Co-author Angela Butler launched *Toolkit* district-wide with a ten-hour summer training program (two hours a day over five days) followed by a five-hour Saturday "refresher" session and four ninety-minute after-school "train the trainer" sessions for reading specialists. (See the orientation session below.) Then she spent the school year visiting and supporting school-centered programs! Your initiative may be significantly less ambitious than Angela's, but the challenges are the same: getting teachers comfortable with the *Toolkit* resources and building a school-based learning community to support *Toolkit* use. To accomplish that, you need time and access to schools and classrooms. Do what you need to do to cajole or negotiate for the time you need to introduce and continue training with the *Toolkits*. It can mean the difference between making a significant impact or not.

Time may be the more important resource to manage, but material resources—books, magazines, Post-its, pads of chart paper, writing and drawing implements, and the like—are important in the *Toolkit* teaching environment. Administrators and teachers need to be convinced that spending precious budget money on these resources (or finding creative ways of acquiring them that don't impact the budget) will pay rich dividends in improved learning. In addition, actions sometimes speak louder than words. Administrative support for reorganizing classrooms, arranging class coverage for teachers observing in-class demonstration lessons, and scheduling planning time to support teacher collaboration can go a long way in making literacy instruction and staff development a school priority.

### Next Up—The Principal!

Whether implementing *The Comprehension Toolkits* district-wide or in a single school or grade level, getting buy-in from the principal and other instructional leaders makes a big difference. During year one of *Toolkit* implementation, plan a one-hour session for all principals to introduce the *Toolkits* and the powerful comprehension instruction that is contained within them. Conduct a slimmed-down version of the comprehension strategies workshop in Chapter 1 to familiarize principals with comprehension strategy instruction and the research-based reasons to teach these strategies:

1. Ask the principals to experience the strategies themselves by reading through an adult piece of short text and discussing, in small groups, the overall meaning of the passage. At the same time, ask them to think about the strategies they used to construct meaning and to consider how those strategies helped them engage more actively in reading and thinking.

2. After principals have read through the text and discussed the meaning with their tablemates, facilitate a group discussion about the meaning of the text, charting the various interpretations. Then ask participants to share the strategies they used to comprehend what they read. Expect these kinds of responses: "I asked questions." "I reread." "I had mental pictures." "I inferred." "I stopped and went back to reread." "I made a connection to my own life." Often principals share the very same strategies *The Comprehension Toolkits* teach. For many administrators this will be the first time they have ever peeled back the layers of their own reading process and noticed what they do to understand what they read. Discussing what they experience—and recognizing that this is what mature readers do to understand what they read—can hook most principals on the *Toolkits*.

3. Solicit the principals' commitment to teachers' participation in the *Toolkit* initiative. Principals are frequently charged with ensuring research-based practice; therefore, it may be helpful to print and share the research articles on the CD-ROM and DVD-ROM and to view the interview with P. David Pearson on *The Comprehension Toolkit* CD-ROM. Encourage the principals to read the articles, and suggest they share them with their staff. Provide a brief overview of the staff development you have planned and the support you need and/or invite them to the orientation session that will

launch your *Toolkit* staff development. Having thought through the time and other resources you need, you'll be able to discuss ways in which the principals can support the effort.

Leadership matters, so getting principals on board makes *Toolkit* implementation far easier than it would be without the active support of these school leaders.

## Introducing the *Toolkits*

There are a few things you will need in order to begin staff development with *The Comprehension Toolkits*:

- Students
- Teachers
- Books, magazines, and copies of short texts
- Desire to develop students who are thoughtful readers and deep thinkers
- *The Comprehension Toolkit* or *The Primary Comprehension Toolkit*

In a nutshell, that really is all you need, but as we've seen, it is much more complex than that. Changing teaching behaviors is especially difficult when it takes people out of the comfort zone they've been in for years. In classrooms where teaching is more of the focus than learning—where teachers, rather than kids, are at the center of the process—*The Comprehension Toolkits* may be an uncomfortable fit at first. *Toolkit* instruction and active literacy ask that teachers gradually release the responsibility of thinking to their students. The *Toolkits* provide specific actions that will assist you and your teachers in releasing the responsibility of thinking and turning over the role of learning to the kids, but many teachers will need to see it before they are comfortable trying it themselves. In essence, they will be looking to you—the literacy coach, the specialist, the trainer—to commit to it first. The rest of this chapter is simply about how to get started communicating that commitment.

### *Starting* Toolkit *Implementation: The Opening Act*

The first step in this long-term staff development effort is to introduce the teaching tools: *The Primary Comprehension Toolkit* and *The Comprehension Toolkit*. You can do this as Angela did, with intensive formal training before teachers even begin the program, or you can provide on-the-go training during the first months that teachers use the *Toolkits* in their classrooms. Training teachers *before* they use the *Toolkits* allows you to prepare them for the challenges they may encounter; training teachers *while* they use the *Toolkits* allows you to tailor your presentation, addressing immediate concerns and meeting the specific needs of teachers.

The three PowerPoint presentations on the accompanying *Staff Development Resources* CD-ROM provide an orientation to the *Toolkits*, and the following section summarizes what you will find there. The first presentation is an overview, suitable for any stakeholder. The next two introduce *The Primary Comprehension Toolkit* (for grades K–2) and *The Comprehension Toolkit* (for grades 3–6). Use either the PowerPoint presentations themselves or the following summaries to plan your own orientation, selecting, revising, or editing the slides to fit your own situation. Whether you use the slides as beginning-to-end presentations or select bits and pieces to illustrate workshops, study groups, or other ongoing training, they provide a basis for understanding the foundations of strong strategy instruction. We have included presenter's notes for your convenience, but feel free to improvise.

### *Giving an Overview:* The Primary Comprehension Toolkit *and* The Comprehension Toolkit

This presentation looks at the following:

- Creating an active literacy classroom
- Defining comprehension and exploring how we best teach it
- Investigating nonfiction literacy

**Part I: Active literacy: What is it, and what does it look like?**
This section defines and describes five key elements of a literate environment:

1. Setting Up a Literate Environment (room arrangement, materials and resources, Post-its, book organization, halls and walls)

2. Creating a Culture of Thinking (text matters, real-world reading, reading for information, strategic thinking and reading, differentiated instruction)

3. Explicit Instruction and the Gradual Release of Responsibility (modeling, guided practice, collaborative practice, independent practice)

4. Social Interaction: Co-Construct Meaning (turn and talk, word talk, anchor charts)

5. Making Thinking Visible (modeling, recording, writing and drawing, displaying kids' work and anchor charts)

### Part II: Reading comprehension strategies in the active literacy classroom

This section begins by asking participants to read an adult text and to reflect on the ways they made sense of it. (**Note**: Taking teachers through the act of analyzing their own reading and thinking—identifying the strategies they use and how and when they use them—will make it easier for them to model and think aloud about the process with their students.) Next, the presenter summarizes the six comprehension strategies that proficient readers use and that are the focus of *Toolkit* instruction:

1. Monitor Comprehension (keep track of thinking, listen to the inner voice, notice when text makes sense or doesn't)

2. Activate and Connect (build background, merge thinking with new learning, change thinking with new information)

3. Ask Questions (ask questions while reading, ask questions to gain information, wonder about big ideas)

4. Infer and Visualize (think of information that isn't explicitly stated, create mental images to construct meaning)

5. Determine Importance (separate important from unimportant facts, identify details supporting larger concepts)

6. Summarize and Synthesize (distill text into a few important details, paraphrase information, move from facts to ideas)

### Part III: Nonfiction literacy instruction

This section begins with some simple classroom management and teaching tips for making instruction with nonfiction texts as effective as possible and ends with a video clip from *The Primary Comprehension Toolkit* DVD-ROM. The video distills the essence of comprehension instruction in a nonfiction-based, active literacy classroom.

### *Introducing* The Primary Comprehension Toolkit: Language and Lessons for Active Literacy

This presentation, designed for teachers and other stakeholders involved in teaching reading comprehension to children from kindergarten through grade 2, introduces *The Primary Toolkit* and is organized around four questions:

1. What's in your *Primary Comprehension Toolkit*?
2. What does a *Primary Toolkit* lesson look like?
3. What does teaching a *Primary Toolkit* lesson look like?
4. How do we assess comprehension with *The Primary Toolkit*?

**Part 1: What's in your *Primary Comprehension Toolkit*?**
This coaching session begins with teachers receiving and exploring their *Toolkit* packages for the first time, and it continues with a brief introduction to each of the components of the kit: strategy books, Teacher's Guide, *Keep Reading! A Source Book of Short Text*, the poster pack of magazines and posters, the "Quick Start Guide," and the DVD-ROM. Finally, the presentation mentions the optional but convenient trade book pack.

**Part 2: What does a *Primary Toolkit* lesson look like?**
This section first walks through Lesson 1 step-by-step from the overview page to the Lesson Guide, pointing out elements common to every *Toolkit* lesson. It then asks participants to read, process, and turn and talk about the lesson, asking any questions they have before the presenter models the lesson or shows a video of a lesson from the DVD-ROM.

**Part 3: What does teaching a *Primary Toolkit* lesson look like?**
After watching a lesson in action, participants turn and talk about what they have seen and then review the lesson's instructional models: Connect & Engage, Model, Guide, Collaborate, Practice Independently, and Share the Learning.

**Part 4: How do we assess comprehension with *The Primary Toolkit*?**
This section begins by showing samples of the ways students demonstrate their thinking in pictures and words: Post-its, thinksheets, anchor charts, and just plain paper. It then discusses ongoing assessment and the various record-keeping devices, rubrics, and tracking sheets that the *Toolkits* provide to support it.

### *Introducing* The Comprehension Toolkit: Language and Lessons for Active Literacy

This presentation, for educators of students in grades 3–6, does exactly what the introduction to *The Primary Comprehension Toolkit* does for K–2 educators, answering these questions:

1. What's in your *Comprehension Toolkit*?
2. What does a *Toolkit* lesson look like?
3. What does teaching a *Toolkit* lesson look like?
4. How do we assess comprehension with the *Toolkit*?

**Part 1: What's in your *Comprehension Toolkit*?**
This coaching session begins with teachers receiving and exploring their *Toolkit* packages for the first time, and it continues with a brief introduction to each of the components of the kit: strategy books, *Teacher's Guide*, *Source Book of Short Text*, *Extend & Investigate*, and the CD-ROM. Finally, the presentation touches on the trade book pack, books in which some of the teaching texts for *Toolkit* lessons can be found.

**Part 2: What does a *Toolkit* lesson look like?**
This section first walks through a lesson step-by-step, from the overview page to the Lesson Guide, pointing out elements common to every *Toolkit* lesson. It then asks participants to read, process, and turn and talk about the lesson, asking any questions they have before the presenter models a think-aloud based on the lesson.

**Part 3: What does teaching a *Toolkit* lesson look like?**
After watching part of the lesson in action (Model), participants turn and talk about what they have seen and then review the lesson's full instructional models: Connect & Engage, Model, Guide, Collaborate, Practice Independently, and Share the Learning.

**Part 4: How do we assess comprehension with the *Toolkit*?**
This section begins by showing samples of the ways students demonstrate their thinking and learning: Post-its, marginal notes, thinksheets, full-page responses, and anchor charts. It then discusses ongoing assessment and the various record-keeping devices, rubrics, and tracking sheets that the *Toolkits* provide to support it.

## Getting Started

The final, and perhaps most important, piece of the orientation training is to inspire teachers to dive in and try out the lessons. Make sure they know that everything they need to get started using the *Toolkits*—lessons, essential language, assessment support, and choice of texts—is included; they may also use additional articles in the *Source Book* (pages 92–135) in the intermediate *Toolkit* as well as the trade book pack. (*Keep Reading! A Source Book of Short Text*, pages 49–137, is in the primary *Toolkit*.) Knowing that everything is included will allow them to focus on the content of the *Toolkits* instead of worrying about any extra work, such as gathering materials, they might be responsible for. Encourage them to read through the first lesson, examine the lesson text, gather their students near, and just have a go at it. Remind them that, like anything new and unfamiliar, the first lesson might feel uncomfortable and that it's not unusual for their students—and even for them—to struggle. But the results are worth it. Suggest that they corral their colleagues—literacy coach, lead teacher, and other teachers at their school who are using the *Toolkits*—to create an on-site support system. Most important of all, commit your own time and effort to providing ongoing support. The orientation training is merely the first step on the journey to higher-level teaching.

## Providing Support

Each workshop begins with an overview of the topic as well as a brief statement of the purpose of the workshop. A materials section lists handouts that you'll need to prepare for each participant: *Toolkit* components such as the teacher's guide or strategy books, other materials that you'll ask your teachers to bring, and any anchor charts or other materials that you'll need to prepare or bring to the session. Then the workshop is laid out step-by-step, with teaching moves and language to guide you as you present the workshop.

Each chapter introduces a topic essential to teaching the *Toolkits*. The Introduction provides background information on the content that you'll cover with your teachers as well as the times when teachers may need support. Each chapter contains the following coaching structures.

Workshops  Workshops—organized and run by a coach based on the needs of teachers—provide time for teachers to learn, discuss, and collaborate with colleagues about the essential elements needed to be successful educators. Each workshop begins with an overview of the topic as well as a brief statement of the purpose of the workshop. A materials section lists handouts that you'll need to prepare for each participant: *Toolkit* components, such as the teacher's guide or strategy books, other materials that you'll ask your teachers to bring, and any anchor charts or other materials that you'll need to prepare or bring to the session. Then the workshop is laid out step-by-step, with teaching moves and language to guide you as you present the workshop.

**Ongoing support**    This section includes detailed information on study groups and in-class coaching. In addition to providing study suggestions for professional texts and topics relevant to the *Toolkits*, the study groups offer suggestions for planning teaching structures, assessing student work, considering needs of different learners, and so on. Most of the study groups in this book focus on the core of the *Toolkits*, including delving into the teacher's guides, looking closely at the strategy books, and investigating other topics that emerge in relation to *Toolkit* instruction and active literacy. In-class coaching is a one-on-one in-class opportunity for a coach to demonstrate or observe a lesson and to provide on-the-spot help. The coaching focus is decided by the teacher and might include using essential teaching language, looking at the amount of teacher talk versus student talk, paying close attention to student engagement, etc.

**Common Core**    A recent development that is well worth noting as you launch *Toolkit* com-
**State Standards**    prehension instruction with your teachers is the adoption by most states of the Common Core State Standards (CCSS). Although the *Toolkits* were published before the standards were made public and adopted, the lessons in *The Comprehension Toolkits* fit like a glove with the K–6 CCSS for informational texts. As a matter of fact, we have found that teachers who are using the *Toolkits* discover that they are already doing much of what the CCSS informational text standards demand. This comes as a great relief to teachers as they work to revise their teaching to meet the new standards.

To support you and your teachers in seeing the relationship between the *Toolkit* lessons and the CCSS, we have created correlation charts for both *The Primary Comprehension Toolkit* lessons and *The Comprehension Toolkit* lessons. These charts are available in Appendix B of this book, and on the *Staff Development Resources* CD-ROM, and can serve as a guide for teachers as they implement the CCSS for informational texts. In addition, a workshop is included in Chapter 1: Comprehension Strategies to support teachers to review the standards and match them to the *Toolkit* lessons that help our kids meet them. Knowing that the *Toolkits* will support them to meet the standards is one more reason to convince teachers to crack open their *Toolkits* and take a shot at implementation.

## Follow-Through with Staff Development

Although formal district- or school-wide presentation is an efficient way to get collective buy-in, one-shot staff development is seldom effective. As a literacy coach, you have as your goal to sustain ongoing interest and effort. The following chapters in this book highlight topics—both learning strategies and teaching methods—that are foundations not only for *Toolkit* teaching but for comprehension across all disciplines. The workshops and ideas for ongoing support through study groups and in-class coaching will give you a starting point for thinking about your own efforts to launch and nourish a collegial environment for professional growth in the schools you serve.

Before implementing the *Toolkits* on a large scale, consider working with one or two teachers to give some of the *Toolkit* lessons a trial run. Trying out lessons yourself will allow you to speak from experience about the planning, teaching decisions, and time involved when beginning *Toolkit* teaching. In addition, these tryouts will yield a collection of valuable student work samples. These artifacts of learning can be used as a basis for discussion with the classroom teachers about student learning—looking at lesson goals and the ways that student responses demonstrate learning, the need for further practice, or the need to reteach. But student samples can also became a powerful piece in the *Comprehension Toolkit* implementation training. Teachers appreciate seeing student responses from children in their own school and district; it makes the *Toolkits* real for them.

Finally, like anything new or different, teachers will have many, many questions as you begin implementing the *Toolkits*. (See the frequently asked questions at the end of each chapter.) Taking a clue from the *Toolkits* themselves, adapt the gradual release of responsibility model to your staff development planning. Plan to provide the most intensive training early in the game by teaching as many demonstration lessons as you can in as many classrooms as you can find teachers to invite you in. The experience will earn a triple payoff. First, you'll engage kids in ways that teachers may not yet have considered. Second, you'll demystify the *Toolkit* lessons for teachers, showing them how to seamlessly engage kids and move from modeling to independent practice. Third, you'll learn a lot and gain credibility with the teachers with whom you work. Teachers want to hear about your challenges as well as your successes and will appreciate hearing, "When **I** was using the *Toolkits*, . . ."

An ongoing focus both on teaching students how to comprehend deeply and on encouraging teachers to reflect on teaching practices and student learning will, in the end, prove to be the most powerful form of staff development. The remainder of this coaching guide will lead you through your own implementation journey. The road will have some twists and turns, maybe even some potholes, but the journey will be worth it—for your teachers and your students.

## Case Study

 For an account of a long-term staff development effort centered on *The Comprehension Toolkits*, check out Joanne Durham's case study in the Afterword of this book as well as on the *Staff Development Resources* CD-ROM in this package. From its beginnings in sowing the seeds for improving instruction to its long-term investment in keeping the interest alive, the installation of the *Toolkits* in Prince Georges County (Maryland) illustrates key principles of exemplary staff development.

**About a month before** our high-stakes state test, I was asked to come in and talk to a group of intermediate teachers (grades 3, 4, and 5) about how they could best use the remaining month of instruction. We looked at the various reading assessments they had collected, including a "mock" state test that allowed the teachers to figure out which of the tested reading tasks—finding the main idea, determining the author's purpose, comparing and contrasting story elements—students had not yet mastered.

I talked to the teachers about the importance of continuing to have students read independently and extensively during the next month, meeting with students in small groups for instruction using texts at their level, and asking students what strategies they used to understand the texts they read. One teacher asked, "What do you exactly mean when you say to 'ask them to tell you how they understand'?"

This was an enlightening question. As a coach, it is the teachers' questions that give me the most information. So I asked them to turn and talk about that, and it appeared that she was not the only teacher wondering about this. Teaching readers to become aware of and consciously use comprehension strategies is at the top of our list when training teachers in *Toolkit* implementation. "Think for a second about the tasks our students are asked to do on the state test," I suggested. "Think, for example, about comparing story elements like characters or events. The concept of taking two characters and showing how they are the same is not difficult if you understand what you are reading. If you don't really understand the text or are only able to comprehend at a surface level, then figuring out how characters are alike becomes much more difficult. In order to understand a text, any text, readers first have to monitor what they are reading by stopping, thinking, connecting, and reacting to the text. Then they may ask questions and create mental images to better understand what they are reading. In order to compare character traits, they would certainly have to use the actions and words from characters to infer what types of characters they are comparing. So in order to do the seemingly simple task of comparing characters, a reader has to do many things first in order to understand the text. If your students are not explicitly aware of the strategies they need to understand the text in the first place, then there is probably little chance they will be successful on the state-assessed tasks."

The room was filled with thoughtful silence for a moment until one teacher looked at me and said, "Hmm. That makes sense. I guess I think I need to rethink my literacy plan for the next month. Do you think it's too late to start talking about this with my kids?"

"Absolutely not," I replied. "It's never too late to talk to children about strategies that will help them think and understand. On Monday, begin asking your students, 'What did you do today in order to understand the text?' Their responses will help guide your comprehension strategy instruction. Most likely you will need to begin with teaching them to monitor their comprehension. Knowing when you understand and when you don't is the first step."

Interestingly enough, two days later I was asked by the reading coach to come back and help train her teachers on *The Comprehension Toolkit*. These teachers had had their *Toolkits* all year, but no one had shown them how powerful the lessons are. Now was the time!

# Introduction

## Comprehension Strategies: What, Why, and When

"Comprehension is not just one more thing. In fact, when it comes to reading, it's the most important thing. If the purpose for reading is anything other than understanding, why read at all?" (Harvey and Goudvis, *Strategies That Work*, 2007)

### *What Are the Comprehension Strategies?*

The research of reading scholars in the last two decades of the twentieth century broke new ground. Researchers began to examine the invisible thinking processes behind reading and thinking. They noted six things that proficient readers do:

1. **Monitor comprehension.** By monitoring their comprehension, they are actively aware of when the text makes sense and when it doesn't, and they take action to repair comprehension when it breaks down.

2. **Activate and connect.** They activate and connect what they already know to the new information they are reading about, adding to and correcting their background knowledge.

3. **Ask questions.** Through asking questions, they seek new information, solve problems, and clarify and extend understanding.

4. **Infer and visualize meaning.** They infer and visualize meaning by drawing conclusions or making interpretations that are not explicitly stated in the text.

5. **Determine importance.** They determine the importance of specific pieces of information in relation to others in the text, sorting details to serve the reading purpose.

6. **Summarize and synthesize.** They take their information and summarize and synthesize it, distilling information to arrive at a big picture and integrating new information to create new ideas.

*The Comprehension Toolkit* is organized around these six key comprehension strategies because their efficacy is clear. Pressley (2002) found that students who were taught these strategies performed better than those receiving more traditional instruction when asked to think aloud about and interpret texts. The explicit lessons in *The Comprehension Toolkits* build understanding of the strategies and provide the crucial teaching language designed to help students learn, approximate, and practice these strategies while reading engaging text.

### When Do Teachers Need Coaching in the Comprehension Strategies?

If teachers are familiar with reading comprehension research or have taught using one of *The Comprehension Toolkits*, some may already understand and use these strategies accurately and well. If, however, they have been concentrating on other areas of reading instruction, on prescribed skills, or on test preparation, a comprehension strategy refresher may be in order.

As you observe in classrooms, ask yourself, "Are teachers and students using the language of comprehension strategies, naming what they are doing when they think about text?" But be aware! You are not looking for parroted terms but for real understanding of the strategies and how they help. Alternatively, when talking to teachers about their reading instruction, ask if their students use and talk about comprehension strategies. If the answers to these questions is "no," consider a coaching session on comprehension strategies.

The following workshop demonstrates how a coach could lead a group of teachers through comprehension instruction in the *Toolkits*. If your teachers study collaboratively or need more individualized attention, see the study group and in-class coaching sections after the workshop for ideas.

# Workshop

## Understanding Comprehension Strategies

When coaching for comprehension strategy instruction, a great place to start is to have teachers experience the strategies themselves. Having teachers observe what they themselves as proficient readers do to comprehend texts allows you to "show, not tell" them how important these comprehension strategies are. You, the coach, can draw their attention to the strategies they used automatically, and then you add to what they already know by teaching them what the strategies are as well as how the *Toolkits* introduce them. Finally, you can move into the idea that students need these same strategies—especially readers who were taught that reading is merely getting the words right and reading them quickly. Once teachers recognize that all readers, including themselves, use the six comprehension strategies to understand texts, they usually become more interested in knowing what they are and how to teach them to their students. As your teachers' curiosity about the strategies increases, so will your ability to talk about, model, and coach for these strategies alongside your teachers.

### Purpose

To experience and notice the strategies we use to understand adult texts, learn what comprehension strategies are, and explore how best to teach them

### Materials

*For each participant:*

- Copy of an adult text that will require participants to think; for example, a one-page nonfiction article, a poem, a short narrative piece. You might use the article titled "Celebration of the Human Voice" by Eduardo Galeano on the overview PowerPoint presentation if you have not already used it with teachers. (See the *Staff Development Resources* CD-ROM.)

- Copy of the "Using Comprehension Strategies" thinksheet (See the *Staff Development Resources* CD-ROM.)

*Ask teachers to bring:*

- Teacher's guide and a strategy book from one of the *Toolkits* (Have teachers bring the *same* strategy book.)

*For the coach:*

- Using Comprehension Strategies anchor chart prepared with two questions:
    1. What was the big idea of the text?
    2. What did you do as a reader to understand the text?
- *Resources for The Comprehension Toolkit* CD-ROM cued to "A Professional Conversation with Dr. P. David Pearson and the Authors—The Three Components of Reading Instruction"

## Workshop Steps

**Share the goals**   Begin this session by distributing the reading text and the thinksheet. Then share the goals of the session: to experience and notice the strategies they use as readers to understand texts, to learn what comprehension strategies are, and to explore how best to teach them.

**Introduce the reading text**   Ask participants to have the adult text you chose in front of them. Connect and engage your participants with the text by sharing a little bit about the text itself and why you chose it. Following are some reasons to choose the text:

- It's topical.
- It's relevant to an experience most people have had.
- It's compelling because of its message.
- It's surprising.
- It's provocative.

After engaging your participants with the text, explain that they will be reading for two purposes today: (1) to get the big idea or the gist of the text, and (2) to think about what they did as readers to understand the text.

Ask participants to read through the text at their own pace and annotate their thoughts and questions in the margin. Suggest that when they are finished, they should jot down what they believe the big ideas were as well as the strategies they noticed themselves using. (You might mention that in the *Toolkits*, this jotting when reading is called "leaving tracks of your thinking.")

**Discuss the text**   Encourage participants to turn and talk (another *Toolkit* practice) to each other about what they read and their thoughts about the text when they are done. (For teachers who aren't used to doing this, you may have to remind them to turn and talk after they have completed the reading.)

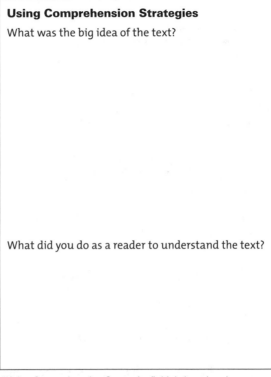

**Using Comprehension Strategies**

What was the big idea of the text?




What did you do as a reader to understand the text?

"Using Comprehension Strategies" thinksheet handout,
available on the Resources CD-ROM

**Record participants' thoughts about what they think the text was mostly about, the big ideas in the text**

When you notice that your participants have had ample time to discuss the meaning of the text with each other and have jotted down their thinking, ask for volunteers to share their ideas. As participants share out, record their thinking on the Using Comprehension Strategies anchor chart (see page 24). Each time a participant provides a response about the gist of the text or the big ideas, ask, "What in the text made you think that?" This is an important question for teachers to experience and begin asking their own students. It will help to uncover the *why* behind their students' thinking.

**Discuss and record the comprehension strategies participants used**

After you've discussed the big ideas, ask teachers to look at their annotations, share what they noticed themselves doing to understand the text, and name the strategies they used to comprehend. Most likely teachers will name the strategies that we find in *The Comprehension Toolkit*: rereading, making connections, asking questions, visualizing, inferring, and often reacting emotionally. If teachers struggle to name the strategies they used, feel free to

What was the big idea of the text?

What did you do as a reader to understand the text?

"Using Comprehension Strategies" anchor chart

restate their ideas in the language of the comprehension strategies: "So you found yourself monitoring your comprehension, making connections, asking questions, inferring, noticing that something was important, summarizing what you learned, and/or putting pieces together and synthesizing what you learned?" Record their thinking and strategy use on an anchor chart.

Once participants have named the strategies they used, point out that none of them named the reading skills usually assessed on the state test (for example, one main idea or author's purpose). That's because those skills are usually a *demonstration* of understanding the text, not what readers do in order to understand the text in the first place. The strategies they use to understand the text are the strategies that the *Toolkits* encompass.

**Define *Toolkit* strategies**   Tell participants that the need for students to learn these strategies is echoed throughout the reading research field. If you have time, begin by showing "A Professional Conversation with Dr. P. David Pearson and the Authors— The Three Components of Reading Instruction" on *The Comprehension Toolkit* CD-ROM. (Dr. Pearson is one of the preeminent initiators of early comprehension strategy research.) Allow participants to turn and talk about what they heard.

Then direct their attention to the summary definitions of the strategies in the *Toolkit* Teacher's Guides (pages 13–14 in *The Primary Comprehension Toolkit* Teacher's Guide; pages 6–7 in *The Comprehension Toolkit* Teacher's Guide). Name each of the strategies, and provide a brief definition of what that strategy entails. Another option is to assign a different strategy to each teacher (or group of teachers, depending on the size of your training audience) to read and share out the information he or she learned about that specific strategy.

**Study how a strategy plays out in a *Toolkit* strategy book**

After reading about each of the strategies, explain that each *Toolkit* has three to six lessons per strategy that gradually build understanding of that strategy, and ask them to turn to the first page of the strategy book you have chosen to study. Explain that every strategy book begins the same way—with basic information to ground them in the strategy. Ask participants to read through the strategy "launch language" found on the first page and to share out what they learned about that strategy.

Then ask participants to work with their tablemates to look at the individual lessons contained in that strategy book. Suggest that they focus on the lesson's Overview (the first two pages of each lesson) and the lesson's Guide (the last two pages of each lesson) to get a sense of the following:

- What the strategy involves
- How strategy instruction is broken down into manageable parts
- How each lesson builds on the previous one

Once participants have had time to read through each of the lesson's Overviews and Guides, ask them to share what they noticed about the strategy, how the *Toolkit* breaks it down, and how the language from each lesson builds on the previous lesson.

**Conclude the session**

Ask the teachers how their new learning might enhance their instruction as well as their students' reading. Remind them that the lessons in the *Toolkits* are strong support for teaching comprehension strategies. They support teachers with teaching language and with pre-selected texts to start with; they support students by engaging them, step-by-step, in the thinking process.

**Note:** You may want to have a sign-up sheet here and at every workshop for any teacher who would like to meet with you individually or would like you to come into her room and model or co-teach one of the lessons with her students.

# Ongoing Support

Choosing to conduct the comprehension strategies workshop, study groups, and one-on-one coaching in a teacher's classroom can add depth to teachers' practices. Following are some ideas for focusing these activities.

## Study Groups

- **Reading comprehension research studies.** There are many seminal studies of reading comprehension research that have had significant impact both on our thoughts about the reading process and on teaching effectiveness. Turn your study group into a reading group. You can either all read and discuss the same article or jigsaw a collection of the best, each one sharing with the others the content of his or her article. There is a great selection of research articles on *The Comprehension Toolkit* CD-ROM, as well as on *The Primary Comprehension Toolkit* DVD-ROM, to get you started.

- **Book groups.** Harvey and Goudvis's *Strategies That Work: Teaching Comprehension for Understanding and Engagement*, Second Edition, provides a professional grounding for all *Toolkit* practices. Chapters 1–5 provide the theoretical foundation and research base for comprehension strategy instruction; Chapters 6–11 provide more multi-genre strategy lessons, giving teachers additional opportunities to support kids' reading of fiction and poetry as well as nonfiction. Consider jigsawing Chapters 6–11, assigning one chapter to each of six teachers and having them share what they learned about strategy lessons and instruction in subsequent study group meetings. Another good book for a comprehension book study is *Comprehension Going Forward: Where We Are and What's Next* (Heinemann, 2011), an edited volume of chapters by authors who are all specialists in comprehension theory and practice. It includes chapters by Debbie Miller, Cris Tovani, and Ellin Keene as well as Stephanie Harvey, Anne Goudvis, and others. The chapters can stand alone, or the book can be read in its entirety. To punctuate the point that we do not teach strategies for strategies' sake, you might suggest that teachers read Steph's chapter "Comprehension to What End?" In it, she describes a comprehension continuum addressing the idea that the goal of comprehension instruction is to use strategies to acquire and actively use knowledge rather than just using them for their own sake!

- **Standards correlations (Common Core State Standards or your district or state standards).** One way to increase your teachers' motivation to embrace comprehension strategy instruction is to help them see the natural connection between the curricular standards and the *Toolkit* comprehension strategies. Support teachers to discover the standards connections themselves. With the recent advent of Common Core State Standards (CCSS), this is even easier as they align beautifully with the *Toolkit* lessons. For example, the Common Core Reading Standards for Informational Text for grades 3–6 ask students to determine the main idea of a text, to explain how it is supported by key details, and to summarize the text. In order to determine the main idea, students first have to identify the most important information and then put those ideas together to discover what the author most wanted the reader to understand. Show teachers how the lessons in strategy books 5 and 6, *Determine Importance* and *Summarize & Synthesize*, support students in determining the main idea(s). In particular, Lessons 18, 19, 21, and 24 teach kids to determine the most important ideas. The Common Core Reading Standards for Informational Text for grades K–2 include a standard related to asking questions. The lessons in the *Ask Questions* strategy book in the *Primary Comprehension Toolkit* play right into this standard. Print the Common Core Reading Standards and *Toolkit* correlation charts from the *Staff Development Resources* CD-ROM and distribute to teachers; then have them review the *Toolkit* lessons in relation to the Common Core Reading Standards with this as a guide. The Common Core Standards for Speaking and Listening also dovetail nicely with the *Toolkit* expectations for student interaction. Encourage teachers to review the Common Core Standards for Speaking and Listening and to notice how the collaboration strategies featured in the *Toolkits*—turning and talking, asking follow-up questions, sharing respectfully, and so on—are linked to the Speaking and Listening standards. Challenge the study group to analyze the standards in terms of the comprehension strategies and then plan their *Toolkit* instruction in relation to the Informational Text and Speaking and Listening standards. Explain to teachers that if they using the *Tookits* faithfully, they are almost certainly meeting most of the CCSS in these two strands.

### In-Class Coaching

- **When students are having trouble with a particular strategy,** help the teacher plan a lesson directed toward helping students grasp it, or teach a demonstration lesson yourself, using the experience both to model effective practice and to diagnose the difficulty students are having. Follow up with a visit to observe the results.

- **When students are grasping strategies easily,** visit the classroom to determine when students are grasping the strategies. Talk to kids. Look for understanding of the current strategy and overall engagement with and understanding of the texts they are working on.

# Frequently Asked Questions

**Do you have to teach the comprehension strategies in order?**

The easy answer to this is "no," although the lessons and the language do build on each other. The *Toolkit* books don't have to be taught in sequence; you can teach what your students need at any given time, tailoring your instruction to what you know about them as readers. For example, if your students have a solid understanding of activating their background knowledge, making connections that enhance their thinking, and merging their thinking with new learning, you may not need to teach the lessons found in the *Activate & Connect* strategy book. If you notice that your students are having a difficult time finding the main idea, you may want to go straight to the *Determine Importance* strategy book. Once you decide which strategy you will be working on, do teach all the lessons in that book in order. The lessons build on each other, providing students with a solid foundation of how to use and approximate that strategy in their own reading.

The following tips may be useful if you decide to vary the sequence of the *Toolkit* lessons:

- Teachers have found that it is generally helpful to begin with the *Monitor Comprehension* strategy book. Monitoring comprehension is more of a thinking disposition than a strategy in and of itself. Once we teach students to be aware of their thinking, they are far more likely to use strategies effectively. So we do encourage teaching kids to monitor their comprehension first and then teaching other strategies in the order best suited to the kids' needs.

- We introduce collaborative practices such as turning and talking throughout various lessons in the *Toolkit*. If you choose a different sequence for *Toolkit* lessons, make sure that you introduce the collaborative practices that are needed for that lesson before you teach the lesson.

- In a similar fashion, we introduce strategy and academic language at different points throughout the *Toolkits*, so make sure you introduce the language needed to do what is required before you teach the lesson.

## Frequently Asked Questions (continued)

■ A final caveat: Teachers have told us that the first time they teach the *Toolkits*, it is helpful to teach the lessons sequentially from the first lesson to the last one to learn the *Toolkit* lessons, language, and practices themselves. That way, when they teach specific *Toolkit* lessons again, they are familiar with them and have a solid idea of their effectiveness at their particular grade level and with their kids. If teachers do choose to go out of sequence when teaching the lessons, point out those lessons that are broken up into two parts, and remind them that those must be done in order.

### How long should I spend on each book?

"As long as your students need to" is usually my response—but with a caution. You don't want to spend so long on a single strategy that it's January before students have the whole arsenal of strategies to bring to their reading. The *Toolkits* were designed to be flexible and allow teachers to use their professional judgment when deciding when to stay with a strategy and when to move on to another strategy. Depending on who your kids are and what they already can do as readers, some strategies will be easier for them to grasp and others will be more difficult; asking questions is often easier for students to do well than determining importance, for example. So you may find that you spend less time working on an easier strategy than a more complex one. An idea to keep in mind is that all students don't learn at the same pace; therefore, when most of the group is ready to move on and only a few students need additional time, you can either meet the needs of those few during small-group instruction or make a note to circle back and teach it again later. Don't forget that the *Extend & Investigate* book (for intermediate grades) offers supplementary thinksheets and language as well as bibliographies for text selection. (Two additional books, *Comprehension Intervention: Small-Group Lessons for The Primary Comprehension Toolkit* and *Comprehension Intervention: Small-Group Lessons for The Comprehension Toolkit*, have been developed to break down each *Toolkit* lesson into smaller lesson chunks to provide extra support for kids who need it. Check them out at www.comprehensiontoolkit.com or www.heinemann.com.)

**I was in a fifth grade classroom** modeling a lesson on how to determine importance. I chose an engaging text about coprolite (otherwise known as Dino Poop from *Toolkit Texts*, Grades 4–5, a great resource for interesting nonfiction articles available at www.comprehensiontoolkit.com), and the students were totally grossed out and completely engrossed in the article. I read the first two sections, thinking aloud as I read about how I determined which sentences were important enough to underline as well as writing my reactions to the information in the margins of the text. As we continued reading for important information, I gradually released responsibility of reading the text to students. I asked them to turn and talk to each other every couple of minutes during the modeling phase. After I completed my demonstration, I suggested they read the last three sections, discuss the text with their tablemates, underline what they considered to be important, and write in the margins what they were thinking about those important parts. The students spent the next ten minutes working together as their teacher and I circulated throughout the room listening to what the students were saying and supporting their thinking when needed. We brought the lesson to a close by charting the important information to remember about coprolite as well as reflecting on and charting what we did as readers to determine important information.

During a post-lesson conference with the teacher, I asked, "What did you notice about your students today?"

She responded, slightly awed, "I noticed that you had them discuss the information more than I usually do and that you asked them to read some parts of the text on their own and jot down their thoughts. They did really well with it. They were definitely engaged, and they were having great conversations. In fact, it seemed that it was the frequent conversations that engaged them in the topic. And all of them stayed on topic, too. I think I need to have them turn and talk more often."

I smiled because learning is a social act and this teacher appeared to be at the beginning of a paradigm shift. She was seeing the "why behind the what" of active literacy. When we ask students to be engaged in text by providing practices to do while they are reading (talking to one another, marking and coding text, collaborating, discussing, etc.), they not only learn more about what they are reading but also learn more about themselves as readers.

I returned to this teacher's classroom about three weeks later. She and the students all had a copy of the same novel. She was reading, and the students were following along. Since we need to expand our reading instruction beyond whole-class novels, I made a "note to self" to talk about the idea of book clubs for reading during our next coaching session. But I was thrilled to see that this teacher was enthusiastically incorporating some of the active literacy practices into her reading instruction. After reading a page to the class, she stopped and said, "Now I want you to read the next two pages. As you read, think about how Jemma has changed since we first began the book. After everyone at your table has had a chance to finish reading, please take some time to discuss her changes."

"*Yes!*" I thought. "*Active literacy in action!*" This teacher was offering more frequent opportunities for her kids to engage in active literacy by interacting with the text and each other. She continued to reflect constantly on her students' engagement level and to collaborate on ways to make her reading block as active and engaging as possible, including book club and literature circle implementation as practices that allow kids to read texts that are at their own level and are of interest to them. Active literacy has ruled the day in this teacher's classroom ever since.

# Introduction

## Active Literacy: What, Why, and When

As the *Toolkit* Teacher's Guides say, "*The Comprehension Toolkit* is not an add-on. It replaces rote fill-in-the-blank activities and worksheets with research-based practices that engage kids and foster active thinking and literacy . . . . *The Comprehension Toolkit* provides an alternative to the traditional assign, memorize, and correct curriculum and encourages, instead, what we call 'Active Literacy.'" In other words, *active literacy* could also be called *engaged literacy*. Students move beyond simply reading and answering questions to reading, thinking, reacting, collaborating, and writing in response to their reading. Active literacy asks students to not only retell what they've read; active literacy asks students what they think and wonder about a text. Active literacy is guided by the idea that, above all, reading is thinking.

### What Is Active Literacy?

Active literacy is brought to life through several instructional practices and conditions that are built into each of the *Toolkit* lessons:

- **Room arrangement.** A comfortable meeting space is available for instruction, desks are in clusters, and tables are arranged so that students can talk to each other.

- **Accessible resources.** Resources, including books, magazines, images, computers, pencils, markers, and Post-its, can be easily located.

- **Think-alouds.** A reader can verbalize his or her thoughts while reading—an "inner conversation" spoken aloud.

- **Text coding.** Students can draw and write symbols in the text while reading as shorthand reminders about their thinking.

- **Annotating.** Jotting quick thoughts in the margins helps students to hold and remember their thinking.

- **Text lifting.** Students can spotlight a section of text for reading, thinking, and discussing.

- **Anchor charts.** Poster-sized records of kids' thinking (and key teaching points) are posted for all to see.

- **Interactive read-alouds.** Oral text reading is interspersed with strategic think-aloud models and discussions.

- **Purposeful talk.** Focused discussion can take many forms—turn and talk, jigsawing, invitational small groups, paired reading, and shares.
- **Guided discussion.** Group discussion is moved along in an intentional direction.
- **Thinksheets.** These graphic organizers scaffold students' thinking about topics and texts.

When teachers are using *The Comprehension Toolkit*, they won't have to figure out how to include active literacy practices in their teaching; they will automatically be using them. Active literacy is a sure thing when using the *Toolkits*! Not every lesson will contain every instructional practice listed above, but each lesson will contain several of the active literacy practices. *Toolkit* lessons are designed to maximize student engagement with text.

### When Do Teachers Need Coaching in Active Literacy?

Active literacy may require the biggest paradigm shift for your teachers. Teachers in conventional classrooms often don't include instructional practices like think-alouds, guided discussion, text coding, or purposeful talk. As educators, we often do what's been done to us, and few teachers grew up in active classrooms like the ones that are so effective today. We teachers also sometimes feel the need to be in control, so we do too much of the work. Teachers work hard—often too hard. The school reformer Harry Wong noted, tongue in cheek, "Schools should not be places where old people go every day to do the work of young people."

The absence of any or many of these active literacy practices is a tipoff that a teacher may need more tools to engage students. But one simple question can provide the most insight into his or her classroom practice: Are your students used to turning and talking? If a teacher sheepishly admits that she doesn't have her kids talk enough, don't despair. As a coach, you can be prepared for any response—no, never, sometimes, or my kids just don't get along. The *Toolkits* offer a great means to turn this around. Fortunately, one of the advantages of *Toolkit* instruction is that it features kids turning and talking throughout and offers the means to turn quiet, complacent classrooms into active, engaging ones.

The *Toolkits* **are** active literacy—from the organization of the lessons, to the gradual releasing of responsibility to students, to the engaging text begging to be discussed as well as coded and marked up, to the thinksheets requiring students to think and respond to text. The *Toolkits* incorporate active literacy into every lesson because reading (and learning for that matter) is a social act. It may take longer with some teachers than others to convince them of the advantages of active literacy, but we have found that once teachers see their students actively engaged in reading and thinking during the *Toolkit* lessons, they will want to adopt the practices of active literacy in all subject areas.

So as you begin working with your teachers on active literacy, support them to get active literacy resources into their classrooms. Make sure that books, magazines, reading texts, and writing tools are all readily available. Look for classrooms with the quiet buzz of collaboration during independent work time as well as plenty of talk during teacher-guided instruction. If these ingredients are in short supply, consider expanding your teachers' arsenal of teaching techniques with active literacy practices.

# Workshop

## Session 1: Observing Active Literacy

For this part of the active literacy workshop, you will be showing the active literacy portion of the video on *The Primary Comprehension Toolkit* DVD-ROM to reinforce what active literacy looks and sounds like.

### Purpose

To observe and reflect on the active literacy classroom

### Materials

*For each participant:*

- Copy of the "Active Literacy Viewing Guide" (See the *Staff Development Resources* CD-ROM.)

*For the coach:*

- Anchor chart from the previous session, "What did we do today that made us actively engaged in our reading?"

- "Active Literacy Slideshow" on the DVD-ROM from *The Primary Comprehension Toolkit* (There is also an "Active Literacy Slideshow" on *The Comprehension Toolkit* CD-ROM if you are working only with intermediate teachers.)

- Anchor chart titled Active Literacy Specialists divided into six sections corresponding to the parts of the "Active Literacy Slideshow": Literate Environment, Culture of Thinking, Explicit Instruction, Social Interaction, Making Thinking Visible, Assessment

- Computer with LCD projector and speakers or DVD player

### *Workshop Steps*

**Turn and talk about student engagement**
Begin today's session by asking participants to turn and talk about the student engagement they noticed since the last session. Have a few participants share out what they noticed.

**Share workshop goals**
Tell participants that today they will be once again looking at active literacy, this time with images and words from real classrooms. Hand out the "Active Literacy Viewing Guide," and ask participants to take a quick look at it. Explain that the slideshow is divided into these sections and that they can use this viewing guide to record any thoughts, questions, reactions, or observations they have as they view each section. If you have participants teaching

**Active Literacy Viewing Guide**

| Active Literacy Component | What am I already doing? | What would I like to incorporate? |
|---|---|---|
| Set Up a Literate Environment | | |
| Create a Culture of Thinking | | |
| Explicit Instruction and Gradual Release of Responsibility | | |
| Social Interaction | | |
| Make Thinking Visible | | |
| Assessment | | |
| Thinking Across the Curriculum | | |

"Active Literacy Viewing Guide" handout, available on the Resources CD-ROM

in the intermediate grades (grades 4–6), suggest that they note ways in which the principles applied here in primary classrooms can be adapted to their classroom environment.

**Show the slideshow**  Show the slideshow section by section, stopping after each one to answer questions and allow discussion. After the group has viewed the entire slideshow, ask teachers to turn and talk with their tablemates about the active literacy practices they most often incorporate in their classrooms. Which ones have they had the most success with?

**Plan active literacy practices**  After discussion, ask each teacher to write his or her name on a Post-it and place it on the Active Literacy Specialists anchor chart in a box representing a practice that is already well established in his or her classroom. Conclude this session by asking teachers to think about which of the remaining strategies they would like to begin incorporating. Ask them to look at the chart to find out who is already incorporating that strategy in the classroom, and encourage teachers to plan time for conversation with that expert or a 20- to 30-minute visit to that expert's classroom to observe the practice in action.

"Active Literacy Specialists" anchor chart

# Session 2: Creating an Active Literacy Classroom

Now it's time to roll up your sleeves! Once you have shown the "Active Literacy Slideshow" in the first part of this workshop and the teachers have had time to process the information, invite a brave teacher to open his classroom after school to get started with a "classroom makeover." Room arrangement is central to active literacy. Kids cannot engage with each other if they are sitting in isolated desks in rows or in any other arrangement not conducive to purposeful talk. Let the teacher know that every teacher in the group will act as a sort of think tank to create a room that is set up for active literacy. Let him know that his willingness to participate in this experiment will result in the bonus of a room ready for active learning.

### Purpose
To arrange a classroom for active literacy

### Materials
*For each participant and the coach:*
■ Clipboard, paper, and pencil for creating room diagram

## *Workshop Steps*

**Diagram an active literacy classroom arrangement**    Meet with all of the participating teachers in the volunteer classroom. Begin by having them look around the room and then visualize how they think the room could be set up for more active learning, keeping in mind what they saw on the "Active Literacy Slideshow." Remind them of the elements of room arrangement featured in the slideshow: a comfortable meeting space and desks in clusters or tables set up so that kids can interact. Have them sketch a diagram of how they would arrange this room—where they would put the meeting space, the desks, the book displays, the accessible resources, etc. Decide together, with particular attention to input from the classroom teacher, how the room should be arranged.

**Rearrange the classroom**    Roll up your sleeves and move the furniture together, arranging spaces for active learning. Set up a comfortable meeting space for explicit instruction; place desks and tables in clusters beyond the space so kids have a place to go during collaborative and independent practice. Place resources, Post-its, pencils, markers, notebooks, etc., in baskets or boxes at the center of tables or desk clusters so kids do not have to wander around the room to find resources.

**Organize resources**    Plan a way to arrange the classroom's remaining books in baskets by genre, author, topic, or general content category. Set up some models, but have the kids help when they are back in the room—they really enjoy classifying texts! Think about placing these book baskets around the room, making sure they are easily seen and accessible. Place a basket of books on a wide range of topics and a variety of levels at the center of each desk cluster or table group so kids can grab a book whenever they have a spare moment to read. Display several books with the covers facing out on the chalk trays, shelves, and other spaces so kids can see the engaging covers. Decide where to put computers and listening centers.

**Wrap up the session**    If possible, schedule teachers' visits to each other's classrooms on the spot, arranging your own schedule to provide coverage for each visiting teacher's classroom. When you have workshops, training, or staff development, bring a calendar and a sign-up sheet as often as possible so you can plan immediately for a follow-up session. As in this session, you don't always have to be the person modeling or demonstrating. Providing coverage while teachers learn from each other is a great way to build collaboration and collegiality. This cannot be emphasized enough. When we offer to cover classes so that teachers can get into other teachers' rooms, we are doing a great service to our teachers!

# Ongoing Support

Each of the active literacy instructional practices in the "Active Literacy Slideshow" can be a session or training in and of itself. Design your own workshops for practices that need follow-up, or organize study groups and in-class coaching.

## *Study Groups*

- **Summarize active literacy practices.** Hand out copies of "How Do We Create an Active Literacy Classroom?" from *The Comprehension Toolkit*, grades 3–6, Teacher's Guide, pages 13–18 (or see the *Staff Development Resources* CD-ROM). Ask participants to number themselves off from one to five, and explain that they will jigsaw this section of the Teacher's Guide, each group reading a section and then sharing its content with the rest of the group. Assign each number to the following sections:
  - 1's—Think-Alouds (pages 13–14)
  - 2's—Text Coding, Text Lifting for Shared Reading, and Anchor Charts (pages 14–15)
  - 3's—Interactive Read-Alouds (pages 15–16)
  - 4's—Purposeful Talk (pages 16–17)
  - 5's—Guided Discussion, Thinksheets (page 18)

  After participants have finished reading their section, ask for volunteers to share out what they learned as they read, making sure to cover each of the sections.

- **Continue with classroom makeovers.** Invite additional teachers to sign up for classroom makeovers—make sure these are volunteers! Once again, invite the group to meet to decide what else is needed to create an environment for thinking. Don't forget to use the topics in the "The Active Literacy Classroom" portion of the "Active Literacy Slideshow" (room arrangement, materials and resources, Post-its, book organization, halls, and walls), or create your own specific criteria when thinking about a classroom makeover. For example, if room arrangement is now more active, focus on a plan for setting up classroom libraries or a structure for organizing accessible reading materials. Ask teachers to volunteer to share something they have done to create a more literate environment, and visit that classroom as a group to celebrate the new space. As you visit these classrooms as a group, be prepared to continue working together on setting up a literate environment, whether it's moving more furniture, arranging more texts, soliciting nonfiction photo magazines from parents, or mounting kids' work on walls and in halls. As a group, you can get a lot done!

- **Use active literacy instructional practices.** Sign up the members of the study group to describe, demonstrate, or provide samples of a particular active literacy practice that has worked well in their classroom: think-aloud, text coding, text lifting, anchor chart, interactive read-aloud, purposeful talk (turn and talk, jigsawing, invitational small groups, paired reading, shares), guided discussion, thinksheet, and so on.

### In-Class Coaching

- **When working with teachers who haven't integrated turning and talking into their teaching practice**, develop a turn-and-talk teaching routine you can use in any classroom you visit. Following is a procedure that has worked in many classrooms across many grades.

  Begin by getting together with the teacher and modeling how you turn and talk to each other. Ask the kids to watch carefully and jot down what they notice you doing. Choose a topic to talk about with the teacher, and have a conversation with each other. Make sure you remember to look each other in the eye, listen attentively, ask follow-up questions, and look and sound interested. Once you have modeled this, ask the students to share out what they notice you doing, and record their thoughts on an anchor chart so they can refer to it when they try it with a partner.

  Then give kids a chance to have a go at it:

  - "Before we get started reading and writing today, let's practice how we turn and talk to each other. Pretend for a moment that today when you walked into the lunchroom, the lady behind the counter said, 'It is your lucky day today. Today you get to order anything in the whole wide world you would like for lunch.' What would it be? Now turn and tell your neighbor what you would order."

  - As students turn to share their lunch orders with each other, observe to make sure that all students have a talking partner. If there is a student who does not have someone to share with, either place partners together or create a triad. And suggest to them that when they turn and talk, they need only to turn their heads rather than rearrange their whole bodies. After a reasonable amount of time (usually about 17 seconds), continue.

- "All right, readers, if everyone in your group hasn't had an opportunity to share, now is the time to let someone else do the talking. Please make sure that you are being a courteous listener."

- After everyone has had time to share with their partner(s), call everyone back together and choose three to four students to share out loud with everyone. After these students share out, summarize what they did that made a successful turn and talk.

- "You guys did an awesome job turning and talking to each other. You took turns, you paid attention to your talking partner, and you discussed the topic we were focused on. Excellent! Today while we read, I am going to be asking you to turn and talk several times. Do exactly what you did just now, and it will be wonderful. Now let's get started."

This procedure is practically foolproof. Providing students a "safe" question that doesn't have a "right" answer allows all students to participate and be successful. And modeling the turn-and-talk process first gives kids an anchor for their own practice. An added bonus is when the teacher tells you in the post-conference, "I wasn't sure my students could do that. They really engaged with one another and had some amazing conversations about what you asked them. I'm going to do this as a regular practice."

■ **When there are a lot of teachers who believe that they should be doing most of the work**, you can expect to see students who are not used to thinking while they're reading (because the teacher usually does most of it). In these classrooms, the teacher and students may be uncomfortable and not immediately successful when first using the *Toolkits*. Your coaching role may be to support, encourage, and cheerlead, pointing out the successful things that students did demonstrate during the lesson. Or you might take a more active role by putting together a demonstration lesson rooted in a surefire, easy-to-read text that is dense with information. Pack your lesson with active literacy teaching practices, and celebrate whatever thinking the students demonstrate.

# Frequently Asked Questions

**I don't like bringing students to the carpet during shared reading because I teach intermediate subjects/they mess with each other/they like to be in their seats. Do I have to do that?**

The easy answer is "no." You don't have to bring kids to the carpet in order to teach with the *Toolkits*. However, lots of experience with *Toolkit* comprehension instruction has shown that kids are far more engaged when they sit up close. I always share with teachers the reason I bring them up close: so I can listen in to what they're discussing and help guide their thinking and my teaching. When I have the children close to me—on the carpet in a group—I have easier access to their reading and thinking. I can fix faulty understanding, add to what they're saying, encourage high-level thinking, and immediately clarify when students misunderstand.

Pulling them to the carpet isn't a magical arrangement that causes students to be successful all of a sudden. It's the idea that they have easy access to each other and each other's thinking that makes the carpet location work. The *Toolkit* lessons will work just fine with kids at their seats as long as two things are occurring: (1) The students are sitting in a way that is conducive to discussion (in small groups, or pairs, or triads), and (2) the teacher is circulating among students to listen in on their thinking and reading.

In addition, just like anything else that we do every day, sometimes you need to change it up a bit. If you normally keep students at their seats, change it up by bringing them to the carpet. If you normally come to the carpet every day, change it up by asking them to collaborate at their seats.

**All those Post-its are expensive and hard to keep track of. Do I have to use them?**

Another easy answer: "No, you don't have to use them." But consider for a moment why they are helpful. First and foremost, Post-its are not as threatening as an entire blank page of notebook paper. A small colored square seems way easier to fill up with thinking than a whole page. Especially for students who are struggling in writing or who hate

## Frequently Asked Questions (continued)

to write, the Post-its are a compromise: You need them to write, and they don't want to, so just have them fill up the Post-it, and you can call it even. Second, for some students, Post-its are just cool—they almost seem grown-up somehow. If giving them a 3 × 3 Post-it square makes them willing to read, think, and write, by all means encourage the use of Post-its. After all, it is a very real-life way of tracking thinking and remembering all the things we need to do. (I carry a Post-it note pad in my purse for the times when I need to jot something down.) Much as pulling them to the carpet isn't a magic bullet, neither are the Post-its. It's what students are being asked to do with the Post-its that makes students actively engaged in reading.

One answer to the expense issue is to substitute copies of a Post-it note sheet, a sheet of paper marked off into boxes in Post-it size. There are a variety of these templates—six-box versions and three-box versions—at the back of the strategy books. Another alternative is to have students take a sheet of notebook paper, draw one line down the center vertically, and draw two or three lines horizontally to create their own "Post-it note sheet."

As for keeping track of the Post-its, almost every lesson opens up the possibility to display a selection of kids' best Post-its on classroom posters or anchor charts. These may show, for example, new learning about a particular topic, facts or responses to a text categorized by thinking process or subtopic, or caption information for a photo or illustration. In addition, save representative Post-its in a child's ongoing assessment record as samples of his or her growing thinking. Send one or two home with an explanatory note celebrating a kid's insight, clever deduction, or summarizing skill to keep parents aware of the work the child is doing. Kids may keep Post-its in notebooks or folders by topic or reading text. And there's one big bonus: Kids' quick thoughts on Post-its are great fodder for writing!

**One bright spring morning** found me in a prebrief conference before a demonstration lesson with five fifth grade teachers, the school reading coach, and the principal. I had been asked to come in and model a *Toolkit* lesson for the fifth grade teachers to give them an opportunity to observe a *Toolkit* lesson as a team and then to have a collaborative discussion about what they noticed and what they wondered. I loved the idea of a collaborative debrief like this, as I suspected that it would generate more questions and discussion than a one-on-one coaching session might. After all, if two heads are better than one, five heads would be exponentially better than two!

I had chosen *The Comprehension Toolkit* Lesson 5, "Merge Your Thinking with New Learning," and I began our prebrief by going over the lesson with the teachers, explaining the lesson goals, the teaching language and moves, and some possible student questions and learning. Next, I shared the lesson text, Stephen Kramer's *Lightning*. As I opened the book, one of the teachers asked me why I chose it. "Are the kids in here studying lightning?" she asked. "I'm just wondering because weather is not a fifth grade unit of study."

And she was right. Weather was not a focus unit in fifth grade. So I began to share my text selection process but caught myself and suggested that all of us keep her question in mind as we experienced the lesson and then address it during the lesson debrief after having watched the kids.

I began the lesson just as described in the *Toolkit* by explaining how important it is to merge our thinking with the text as we read and to listen to the voice in our head that signals new learning by paying attention to inner phrases such as "Wow, I never knew …," "No way," or "That's surprising." Once

I felt they had at least a grasp of the focus strategy of the lesson, I pulled out the book. The cover alone captures readers with the bold, italicized Lightning title and the striking photo of a crackling web of sky-to-ground lightning. I continued to flip through the pages, many of which featured amazing photographs of lightning in every imaginable context—above cities, in the clouds, over the ocean. The kids were oohing and aahing as if it were the Fourth of July and we hadn't yet read a page. Then in a hushed voice, I read the first page:

> Late in the evening, a dark cloud hangs in the sky. The air is calm. The birds are quiet. Even the blades of dry grass are still. Everything is hushed, waiting. Suddenly a giant spark leaps through the air, connecting earth and sky. The spark flickers for an instant and disappears. There is a moment of silence. Then a tremendous crack rips through the quiet. Booming echoes follow, rolling across the land. A thunderstorm drifts across the summer sky.

You could hear a pin drop when suddenly a voice broke the silence: "It sounds like poetry!" And he was right, of course. It did sound like poetry because Stephen Kramer writes lively, compelling, vivid nonfiction that knocks your socks off. We read a few pages more, stopping and jotting our new learning throughout. Then I turned to the table of contents and explained that one of the things I loved about nonfiction is that you don't always have to read it in order. I shared the section headings and let them turn, talk, and choose where to go next. The consensus choice was a section toward the end of the book called "Fascinating Facts." A spirited discussion with connections, questions, and inferences ensued as we read, jotted, and talked about some amazing facts about stormy weather. It was spring and there were thunderstorms aplenty, so the kids had lots to talk about. The lesson was over before we knew it, and a dozen kids were clamoring for the book as they headed out to recess.

As we began the post-lesson debrief, the teacher with the text question opened immediately. "Now I understand the choice of text. It was so well written the kids couldn't get enough of it. They were so engaged throughout. We need to find texts in our content areas that are as compelling as that *Lightning* book."

"And reading the text out of order was an insight for me," another teacher weighed in, "and a terrific way to engage them in the topic. You could see at the end with all of those kids crowded around that they were hungry for more information."

"I love nonfiction," said a third teacher, "but I'm thinking I don't read it out loud enough."

An energetic collaborative discussion on how and why to choose a text ensued. Choice of text matters. Text is central to student engagement and learning, so spending time figuring out how to choose it, planning how to use it for teaching, and supporting teachers to do so are essential for good, solid, engaging comprehension instruction.

# Introduction

## Text Selection: What, Why, and When

Text matters—a lot! If kids are not reading engaging, interesting, thought-provoking texts, why should they bother? If we're going to ask kids to think critically and hard about a text, then we need to give them a text worth thinking about. When students read texts that raise significant issues and provoke thinking, they become active readers. As I often tell my teachers, "There are too many great books, even just good books, for kids to be reading junk!"

### What Is Text Selection?

Choosing appropriate texts around which to center comprehension instruction requires thoughtful judgment, balancing content interest, concept difficulty, and application of comprehension strategies. *The Comprehension Toolkits* provide engaging, interesting, thought-provoking nonfiction texts for every lesson in the form of a book or magazine text. Additional short texts in the source books in each kit and a set of texts in English and Spanish in separately available *Toolkit Texts* volumes provide a sound foundation. You do not want your teachers to stop there, however. In the end, a teacher should be able to select a variety of engaging texts to help kids read and understand. The "Text Matters" section at the beginning of every lesson provides a rationale for selecting that particular text for that particular strategy lesson. Helping teachers generalize from these rationales and learn how to think about the texts they choose for their teaching can extend the value of *Toolkit* lessons far beyond the texts available with the program. Coaching with the *Toolkits* can help your teachers evaluate nonfiction teaching selections for interest and instruction.

### When Do Teachers Need Coaching in Text Selection?

As you work with teachers in implementing the *Toolkits*, you'll quickly pick up on any anxiety around text selection. If you are hearing questions like "What if my students can't read the provided text?" and "What if my kids already read that text last year?" you will know you have helped them rethink the way they are looking at text selection. The following workshop and alternative supporting coaching sessions familiarize teachers with ways to let the read-aloud set up the thinking and support them to select texts that are developmentally appropriate to their students' backgrounds, skill levels, and interests. Most teachers will use the text that the *Toolkits* provide at first, and as a coach, I typically encourage teachers to do so. Much thought has gone into the selection of the texts used in the *Toolkits*—quality writing, high-interest topics, and opportunities to practice the focus strategy—so teachers can feel comfortable that students will be reading great texts. Ultimately, though, you want them to recognize what it takes to select appropriate texts for instruction and move toward them selecting their own texts.

As you observe in classrooms, ask yourself, "Are the texts kids are reading interesting to them?" and "Are they age-appropriate and suited to the teaching goal?" and "Are they all the appropriate reading level?" You should be able to see readers sharing what they are reading, responding with eagerness to the content, talking about ideas in the text. Be alert to teachers' responses when you ask if their students like to read nonfiction. A "no" answer may be a hint that the match of text to reader is not optimal, another signal that a coaching session on text selection might be a good idea.

# Workshop

## Session 1: Developing Text Selection Criteria

The *Toolkit* philosophy and practices are most effective when teachers adapt the lessons as part of their own curriculum, texts, and instructional goals. This two-part workshop begins with an analysis of the text selection process in a variety of *Toolkit* lessons. First, participants examine "Text Matters" sections in a range of *Toolkit* strategy books as a springboard to developing their own text selection criteria. In the second session, teachers evaluate and choose their own texts to plan teaching for an upcoming *Toolkit* lesson. At this point, teachers can truly make *Toolkit* practices their own by sharing texts they are enthusiastic about that will excite and engage the kids in their classrooms. In the two workshop sessions, participants will do the following:

- Explore and analyze how texts were chosen for instruction throughout the *Toolkits*.

- Generate criteria for selecting texts based on teaching goals and purposes as well as on student learning needs and interests.

- Evaluate and select texts for instruction.

- Match various forms of explicit instruction to their instructional goals as they plan lessons with selected texts.

### Purpose
To explore and analyze how texts are chosen for instruction throughout the *Toolkits* and to generate criteria for selecting texts

### Materials
*Ask teachers to bring:*
- *Toolkit* Teacher's Guide (either primary or intermediate)
- All the strategy books from their *Toolkits*

*For the coach:*
- Chart for recording criteria for text selection

### *Workshop Steps*

**Share the goals**   Explain that in this workshop, teachers will familiarize themselves with texts across a range of *Toolkit* lessons. This is an opportunity to explore the variety of texts used to teach many different strategies, from making connections to questioning to summarizing and synthesizing. A great deal of thought has gone into the texts selected for specific lessons, and teachers will examine lessons to pull out and create criteria for selecting their own texts.

**Discuss the principles behind *Toolkit* text selection**

Direct participants' attention to the "How Do We Choose and Use Text?" section in their *Toolkit* Teacher's Guide (*The Primary Comprehension Toolkit*, pages 48–49; *The Comprehension Toolkit*, pages 41–42). Jigsaw the reading, assigning each section to a participant, pair, or group. After reading, have them share out and discuss. Which text selection principles are most important to your students?

Continue with the same groups, asking them to examine the "Text Matters" sections in different strategy books. Direct them to note why and how the texts were chosen.

**Co-construct a list of criteria for choosing texts**

Create a chart titled Criteria for Text Selection. As participants share out what they have learned from "Text Matters," use the why's and how's they share to begin a list of general criteria for text selection, adding to them as the group considers other factors. The criteria might include the following:

- Accurate, clearly explained information or narrative
- Many opportunities for the teacher to model his or her own thinking, and use of the focus strategy as well as other strategies
- Content and style that encourage use of a particular strategy—asking questions, making inferences, sorting and sifting information
- Interesting, engaging format, illustrations, and features
- Engaging writing style, unique perspective, or striking information
- Substantive ideas and issues that provoke thinking and discussion
- Enough background information (that students already have or that we can provide) so that students can understand the lesson as it unfolds with this text
- Attributes that relate to the goals and purposes of lessons, such as unfamiliar facts in a lesson on asking questions about new information
- Relationship to an ongoing topic or unit of study—or connections to science and social studies curriculums—to maximize background knowledge and depth of understanding

**Create a text selection guide**  Consider turning the criteria into questions to be considered as participants seek out their own texts. Is the text well written and accurate? Will the text engage my students? How will I build my students' background knowledge so that the text content will be comprehensible to them?

# Session 2: Selecting Texts and Planning a Lesson

This session will give participants an opportunity to work together to read, evaluate, and select their own texts and then to consider explicit options for instruction as they begin to plan their own lessons. Before the session, find out some of the upcoming lessons that teachers will be teaching, and gather books, articles, and online resources that might be appropriate for these particular lessons. Ask teachers to prepare for the workshop by bringing in three or four texts they have found to be good matches for upcoming comprehension instruction. If the texts are connected to ongoing themes or curricular topics, so much the better!

### Purpose

To work together to read and evaluate texts, use the text selection criteria to choose texts for instruction, and plan a lesson

### Materials

*Ask teachers to bring:*

- *Toolkit* Teacher's Guide (either primary or intermediate)
- Strategy book containing the lessons they are planning to teach next

*For the coach:*

- Chart of criteria for text selection
- Lots of books and resources—picture books, trade books, realistic fiction and nonfiction, short articles, the *Source Book*, *Keep Reading!*, and other sources of text such as *Toolkit Texts* (if available)

### *Workshop Steps*

**Share the goals**  Explain that in the first half of this session, participants will be reading, reviewing, and discussing a variety of texts and selecting the most appropriate for upcoming strategy instruction. The selection will conclude with collaborative planning—in pairs or small groups—of a lesson based on the chosen text.

**Review the criteria for text selection**

Display the chart developed in the last session. If any teacher has chosen a text since the last session, ask how it went. Was the text successful? Did it engage students' attention? Was it appropriate for getting across the instructional focus of the lesson? Why or why not? The discussion may yield additional criteria for your list or clarifications of existing criteria on your list.

**Evaluate and select texts**

Group participants according to the lesson or strategy they will be teaching next. Ideally, two or more teachers will be able to work collaboratively selecting texts and planning instruction for the same lesson. If this is not the case, attempt at least to group those who are teaching from the same strategy book. In this way, teachers can support each other to locate selections appropriate to their particular strategy focus.

Invite the groups to quickly review the lesson they will be teaching (or select one arbitrarily if they are at different points in their teaching), and then delve into the texts they brought as well as those you have provided to locate a text appropriate to that lesson. Encourage participants to judge the texts against their list of text selection criteria and to consider the pros and cons of several different texts for teaching their particular lesson. Provide time for them to bring up questions or issues related to the texts and the lessons. Finally, have the group agree on a text or texts to be used to plan the chosen lesson.

**Review instructional options for teaching with texts**

Once participants have selected texts, ask them to keep those texts in mind as they review the different teaching structures—thinking aloud, text coding, text lifting for shared reading, interactive read-alouds, and the like—described in their Teacher's Guide in *The Primary Comprehension Toolkit*, pages 23–25, and in *The Comprehension Toolkit*, pages 13–16.

**Determine how to share the text with students**

As they begin to plan their lessons, direct groups to first consider the best way to share the text they have chosen with their readers. Remind participants to be sure to match the text, the instruction, and the lesson goals and to consider how accessible and comprehensible the text is for their particular group of students in addition to the other criteria. Ask these questions:

- Does the text lend itself to an interactive read-aloud when a good part of the book is read aloud and the students respond on Post-its during the reading? Narrative nonfiction and realistic fiction are often good choices for interactive read-alouds.
- Does the text lend itself to a text lift, when a smaller portion of the text is projected so the teacher can model with think-alouds and

annotations? Shorter or less challenging texts that students can complete themselves lend themselves to this approach.

**Create a think-aloud using the Lesson Guide** Direct participants' attention to the Lesson Guide at the end of their lesson where they will find some generic teaching language they can adapt for use with the text they have selected. Have each group script or outline the teaching language—and the specific examples from their text—they will use to work with their students on the strategy. (See Chapter 6 for expanded development of think-alouds.)

**Present a lesson** Ask groups to share the lessons they planned. Try to see that both interactive read-alouds and text lifts are represented. The think-alouds are likely to look a bit different in each case. This presentation doesn't need to be a full-blown demonstration but can instead be a summary of the thinking that went into their planning:

- What text they chose and why
- How the think-aloud to model the strategy would go
- How to use the lesson guide as a support with the alternate text

**Create a list of alternative texts for specific *Toolkit* lessons** End the session by asking teachers to share texts that worked well in their lessons (as well as ones that did not!) and those that looked promising during their early review. Compile a list of recommended teaching texts; pay particular attention to creating lists that work well with content topics in science and social studies. Finally, ask participants to reflect on how they view texts differently as a result of this workshop.

# Ongoing Support

### *Study Groups*

- **Nonfiction libraries.** Gather participants in grade-level teams, and pay a visit to the bookroom or library, wherever books for guided and independent reading are stored in the school. If books and materials are scattered throughout the school, it's a good time to do a little reconnaissance and figure out exactly what the school has and where all the "stuff" is located! Help teachers think about their students' independent reading levels, and make sure that their classroom includes books well "below" and "above" these levels. Choose texts by interest as well as by reading level.

  Support teachers to find interesting magazine articles and other short texts (see the *Toolkit Text*s and the *Toolkit Source Books* as well as the bibliographies on pages 125–139 in *Extend & Investigate* and on pages 139–155 in *Keep Reading! A Source Book of Short Text*) to use both for instruction and for independent reading. Flood the rooms with a great variety of texts at many different levels on a wide range of topics.

- **Text talks.** As teachers begin examining additional texts to use with the *Toolkit* lessons, encourage conversation with other grade-level teachers as well as those in the grades above and below. Convene a children's "book group," and adapt the traditional book talk—sharing thumbnail sketches of books to help readers choose what to read—to a text talk. Ask each participant to bring three to five engaging, age-appropriate nonfiction texts to share. Provide a simple presentation template (see "Text Talk" on the *Staff Development Resources* CD-ROM for an example), and send participants off with your promise to compile a list of the texts that were shared. There's no better way for teachers to plan together and find new texts that enliven their *Toolkit* lessons. In addition, engage kids in nonfiction authors' studies the same way we often do with fiction. Some great nonfiction authors worth investigating include Stephen Kramer (the writer of the book noted in the opening vignette for this chapter), Nicola Davies, Seymour Simon, and Kathryn Laskey.

- ***Toolkits* and content areas.** The *Toolkit* nonfiction focus emphasizes how important it is for students to "read to learn" all day and every day, building a repertoire of reading strategies that are tools for learning in different disciplines. The lessons and practices are the perfect vehicle for showing teachers how to bridge reading and the content areas. (You will be meeting the Common Core State Standards to boot!) Convene a study group to research and compile a bibliography of picture books, trade books, articles, and resources that teach important concepts and support grade-level topics in science and social studies and that foster active learning in ways that science or social studies textbooks can't. Invite your school or local librarian to join you and to share his or her expertise. Search online; input topics into Amazon.com, and read the summaries and reviews. Finding texts that match the grade-level social studies and science standards will allow teachers to teach reading and thinking strategies across the curriculum and help children learn specific content. See Chapter 7, "Content Literacy Across the Curriculum," for more on using the *Toolkits* in the content areas.

### In-Class Coaching

■ **Survey the nonfiction resources in a teacher's classroom.** With the teacher, evaluate the range of available materials (books, magazines, posters, realia) and their suitability to the classroom (appropriateness of topics, difficulty, interest level, curriculum match). Brainstorm ways to add to the collection or to redistribute materials that might fit better into another classroom. (Organize a book swap!)

■ **After observing a lesson, discuss it with the teacher.** Ask how he or she might use texts more flexibly and purposefully to explicitly teach comprehension strategies. Look back at the criteria for text selection, and consider the following questions:
  • Were students engaged with and interested in the text?
  • How might you vary how you used this book with the lesson next time?
  • How might children's thinking have been extended with this text?
  • Were children able to practice using the strategy or strategies during guided practice with this text?
  • What other texts might have worked even better with this lesson than the book/article selected?

# Frequently Asked Questions

**If the teachers at our school are using *The Comprehension Toolkit* in grades 3, 4, and 5 or K, 1, and 2, won't they have seen the text already? Then what will we use?**

This is without a doubt *the* most frequently asked question about texts and the *Toolkits*. The *Toolkits* come with a variety of texts, magazine articles, and trade books, and the *Toolkit* lessons themselves are meant to be taught over and over again with different content, different texts, and different contexts. We believe that kids need to read with a question in mind when reading fiction and nonfiction as well as science and social studies. However, we do not advocate that every teacher teach the same lesson again with the same exact text. So we spend time teaching teachers to use different texts for different *Toolkit* lessons and for different purposes (as we suggest in this chapter).

The most important two-page spread in the strategy books is the Lesson Guide, which comes at the end of each *Toolkit* lesson. This guide strips away the text and the content from the entire *Toolkit* lesson and leaves just the generic teaching moves and teaching language. We suggest that teachers use this as a support to teach the *Toolkits* with different texts. For example, on the *Primary Toolkit* DVD-ROM, a video shows Steph teaching Lesson 7, "Merge Thinking with New Learning," with an alternative text to the one actually used in the *Toolkit* lesson. Encourage teachers to take a look at this video clip to see how a *Toolkit* lesson can be taught with a different text.

One caveat: Often teachers are most comfortable using the designated lesson text the first time they do the lesson. This is natural and helps teachers fully understand the *Toolkit* practices. In addition, Scott Paris talks about the importance of students revisiting a text. Each time a reader revisits a text, he or she is likely to understand it in a different and often deeper way. For example, *The Mary Celeste: An Unsolved Mystery from History* (intermediate *Toolkit* Lesson 7) and *Titanic* (intermediate Lessons 10 and 11) are filled with exciting information from the first to the last page. Students beg to keep reading these texts again and again. In fact, acknowledging that rereading a text is an important part of becoming a proficient reader engages those students who may feel

## Frequently Asked Questions (continued)

they have nothing new to learn from a text they have already listened to and read. The overall point of *Toolkit* comprehension instruction is that you choose a text that serves your purpose and the purpose of the curriculum and—most importantly—that best meets your students' learning needs and interests and then use the lesson guide to help you teach the lesson with a different text.

### Can I use *Toolkit* lessons and practices with the textbook?

A resounding "yes!" If there's one kind of material that requires kids to really sort and sift information, ferreting out what's important to remember, it's the information-overloaded textbook. Many of the lessons involving determining importance and summarizing and synthesizing teach note-taking strategies that work well with textbook content. Two lessons in the intermediate *Toolkit*'s "Determine Importance" unit (Lessons 18 and 19) use a textbook chapter on the American Revolution, but of course it makes the most sense for you to use your own textbook for these lessons. You'll find additional suggestions for many more lessons with textbooks in the intermediate *Toolkit*'s *Extend & Investigate* book. The section titled "The Genre of Textbook Reading" (pages 23–73) suggests various alternatives to answering the questions at the end of the textbook chapter and recommends an arsenal of strategies and lessons for more thoughtful approaches to reading and learning from these tomes.

And last but not least, don't forget that both *Toolkits* provide a wealth of sources for alternative texts:

■ Collections of short nonfiction texts. See pages 49–137 in the *Keep Reading! Source Book* in the primary kit and pages 91–135 in the *Source Book of Short Text* in the intermediate kit.

■ Suggestions for where to look for authentic texts. See the bibliographies on pages 139–155 of the primary *Keep Reading! Source Book* and pages 125–139 of the intermediate *Extend & Investigate* book.

*Toolkit Texts*, a collection of nonfiction articles at a variety of reading levels—grades preK–1, 2–3, 4–5, and 6–7—are available at www.comprehensiontoolkit.com.

**Three years ago**, I took a ballroom dancing class with my friend Stephen; we were signed up to learn the waltz, fox-trot, and merengue. I was totally excited! In college I had been a dancer and had a pretty good command of the dance floor. Essentially, I had a lot of background knowledge and was a "good dancer." Stephen, on the other hand, did not have a lot of background knowledge and was a "dancer at risk." He was willing to go but was not overly confident in his ability to learn the merengue. Surprisingly, as we left that first dance class, we were both impressed with how well he did, and it dawned on me as we drove home that our dance instructors had used the gradual release of responsibility to teach him the dance.

Our dance instructors (the cutest 80-year-old couple) began the class by asking us to stand along the edge of the dance floor and watch as they gave us a (1) **demonstration**, or a model, of the merengue. As they moved effortlessly along the parquet floor, they would think aloud about the moves they were making: "Left hand on hip, right hand on shoulder, hips square. Left foot front. Cha-cha-cha. Right foot front. Cha-cha-cha." Then they slowed down the dance and walked slowly through each step. After that, they invited us to join them on the dance floor. They provided (2) **guided practice** as we began approximating their moves. Stephen and I were responsible for think-ing through the moves and moving our feet, arms, and shoulders at the right time. When the instructors saw us either moving incorrectly or being unable to remember what to do next, they would step in and provide support. After they guided our practice, the instructors moved to the outside of the dance floor and allowed the couples to work together in a form of (3) **collaborative practice**. We watched the other couples for technique, and we often asked each other, "What move comes next" "Which foot goes first?" Before we left, the instructors played two or three songs so every couple had time for (4) **independent practice** before we left for the night. The expectation for each of the couples in the class was that we would practice the dance at home, and the next time we went dancing, we were to use an (5) **application** of the strategy by dancing the merengue. Our instructors' use of the gradual release of responsibility worked for both "good" and "struggling" dancers. The same is true for readers when using the *Toolkits* and their gradual release of responsibility framework. It works.

# Introduction

## Gradual Release of Responsibility: What, Why, and When

"I do, you do" is the *sudden* release of responsibility, whereas "I do, we do, you do" is the *gradual* release of responsibility (Pearson and Gallagher, 1983). Teachers are famous for working hard. We teach our hearts out and desperately want all children to succeed. Very often while we're teaching children to read, we take on the lion's share of the work—we do the reading, we do the talking, we do the thinking. Then, when it's time for the students to work independently, they often struggle trying to remember what the teacher did. The students move from listening or watching the teacher do something to trying to do it themselves ("I do, you do"). The missing piece is the doing it together ("I do, *we do*, you do"). In fact, sometimes the scenario is missing two parts, the modeling ("I do") and the guided practice ("we do"). In this case, explaining and assigning ("you do") is the teaching approach. (See Chapter 5, "Modeling: Think-Alouds and Demonstrations," for coaching sessions.) The gradual release of responsibility defines almost every successful learning experience, whether it is reading, dancing, or learning to play tennis.

### What Is the Gradual Release of Responsibility?

When thinking about pedagogy and best practices in learning, the gradual release of responsibility (GRR) method is probably the most effective teaching framework. First of all, it just makes sense; second, the research supports it. In a nutshell, the GRR instructional model involves the intentional shifting, over time, of the responsibility for performing a task from the teacher to the student.

In every lesson in the *Toolkits*, you'll find a predictable five- or six-part teaching structure (either item 4 or 5 can be used or both items 4 and 5 can be used) that reflects the GRR:

1. **Connect & Engage.** The teacher piques students' interest and activates and explores their background knowledge.

2. **Model.** The teacher provides explicit instruction, demonstrating the strategy and thinking aloud to make the invisible cognitive processes underlying the strategy clear.

3. **Guide.** Students begin trying out the strategy with support from the teacher.

4. **Collaborate.** The students perform the strategy together in pairs or small groups while the teacher circulates, conferring with partners or small groups.

5. **Practice Independently.** The students perform the strategy on their own while the teacher circulates, conferring with individuals.

6. **Share the Learning.** Students share their responses—what they have discovered, and how they have discovered it (strategy use)—with the teacher acting as moderator.

The GRR model relies on conferring—checking in with students during collaborative or independent practice—to ensure its success. In a brief conference, a teacher can find out what the student knows, determine what he or she needs, and determine how to give that help—a brief reminder or prompt on the spot or an additional minilesson in a small group or for the class. When students are practicing—especially right after a strategy lesson—teachers must be as fully engaged in the practice as the kids. This is not the time to correct papers or plan the next day's instruction or even pull a small group for unrelated instruction. This is the time to hone your listening and instructional problem-solving skills in a conference to diagnose and address where each student is, where he or she needs to be, and how you will get him or her there.

The GRR model in the *Toolkits* applies to the choice of texts as well as to the instructional framework. When you begin a new strategy, the *Toolkits* provide a highly supportive text for teaching that strategy. As students become more successful with the strategy, opportunities are provided to tackle more challenging texts. For example, for determining importance, the intermediate *Toolkit* first provides text that is sectioned off by subheads, which make it easier to determine the big ideas, and then moves into material that does not have subheads. The primary *Toolkit* relies on increasingly sophisticated pictorial posters to teach the same skill.

## When Do Teachers Need Coaching in the Gradual Release of Responsibility?

For many teachers, the gradual release of responsibility is one of the most difficult concepts to grasp—not because it is a difficult concept to understand, but because they have never taught like that. Remember the observation that teachers work hard, so hard that they do all the work? They do. So when we talk to them about letting go of some of the responsibility for the lesson to students, they feel as if they are not doing their jobs if they are not directing students. As a coach, it is your job to remind them that their job is not to do all the work (teachers already know how to read); rather, their job is to prepare their students to do the work of learning to read and to nudge them along the road to success. Their role is one of explicit modeling: showing students how to use the focus comprehension strategy followed by consistently conferring, monitoring kids' learning, and providing gentle support as they perform.

Look for signs of the GRR model in your classrooms: Do teachers consistently engage kids' enthusiasm and background knowledge from the beginning? Do they provide a model and guide whole-group practice before handing over responsibility to kids? Do they allow time for practice—either collaborative or independent—and reflection? Do they confer with students throughout the practice to provide the support they need? Missing any stage in the process may signal pacing problems, moving either too fast (skipping steps in the GRR model) or too slowly (getting hung up on one or more steps), or the lack of strong scaffolding for students who need it. Grounding in the GRR model will strengthen instruction in these classrooms.

# Workshop

## Session 1: Understanding the Gradual Release of Responsibility Model

Most likely the first thing you will need to do when coaching toward the gradual release of responsibility model is to walk your teachers through (1) what it is, (2) why it's important, and (3) how it works in the *Toolkits*. A coach's role is multifaceted, but two of our primary responsibilities are to constantly search for best practices and to understand why they are best practices. When we provide teachers with the rationale for certain teaching practices, teachers will be able to reflect more deeply on their teaching decisions and understand the implications for student learning. This initial gradual release of responsibility discussion can occur during an in-service training with multiple grade levels, with individual grade-level teams, or with any group of teachers unfamiliar with the GRR framework.

### Purpose

To observe the gradual release of responsibility teaching model in action and explore how it is utilized throughout the *Toolkits*

### Materials

*For each participant:*

■ Copy of the "Gradual Release of Responsibility Note-Taking Grid" (See the *Staff Development Resources* CD-ROM.)

■ Copy of the "Gradual Release of Responsibility Viewing Guide" (See the *Staff Development Resources* CD-ROM.)

*For the coach:*

■ Video from the "Comprehension in Action: Three Classroom Videos" section of *The Primary Comprehension Toolkit* DVD-ROM

■ Summary of gradual release of responsibility teaching steps from one of the *Toolkit* Teacher's Guides: *The Primary Comprehension Toolkit* Teacher's Guide, page 10, and/or *The Comprehension Toolkit* Teacher's Guide, page 24

## Workshop Steps

**Share an example**

When introducing the gradual release of responsibility model to your teachers, share a personal anecdote of a time when you learned something new—a dance, a tennis stroke, a new way to make an old family recipe—when the learning followed the steps of the gradual release of responsibility. (See the introductory vignette for an example.) It doesn't matter what the skill is; the important part is illustrating to teachers the effectiveness of the GRR model.

After you've shared your personal experience, have your teachers take a moment and reflect on something they've learned to do. Encourage teachers to think outside the world of school because it requires them to think more deeply and makes the conversation more interesting. Ask them to think back to how they learned to do that hobby and to quickly write down the steps. Invite teachers to share with their tablemates the steps they remember.

**Define *gradual release of responsibility,* and share workshop goals**

After teachers have had time to discuss, explain that most of them probably learned through a combination of steps: someone modeling or demonstrating how to do it, someone guiding them through the steps, and practicing a lot. This collection of teaching steps—from instructor controlled or teacher controlled to learner controlled—is called the gradual release of responsibility, and it provides a framework for learning that meets the needs of both proficient and struggling students. Tell them that today they'll be seeing how the gradual release of responsibility supports the teaching of comprehension.

**Study the *Toolkit* lesson framework**

Hand out the "Gradual Release of Responsibility Note-Taking Grid" (see the *Staff Development Resources* CD-ROM), and briefly discuss the general steps in the framework, connecting the steps they outlined for learning their personal sport or hobby with the steps in the framework. Allow time to read and discuss each step.

Then ask teachers to take out any strategy book and page through it, noting the lesson structure on the grid and how that structure is reflected in the Lesson Guide at the end of every lesson. Guide teachers to note how the lesson structure reflects the GRR structure, noticing the lesson steps next to the GRR model descriptions.

**Demonstrate or show a video of a gradual release lesson**

To make the GRR model real for your teachers, show them what it looks like in action by using a classroom video from *The Primary Toolkit* DVD-ROM or by demonstrating a lesson yourself, using teachers as students and calling attention to the gradual release stages as you teach.

## Gradual Release of Responsibility Note-Taking Grid

| Gradual Release of Responsibility Framework<br>Adapted from Fielding and Pearson (1994) | Toolkit Lesson Structure |
|---|---|
| **Connect and Engage**<br>Teacher activates students' prior knowledge and engages their interest. | |
| **Teacher Modeling**<br>Teacher explains and models the strategy with demonstrations and think-alouds. | |
| **Guided Practice**<br>Teacher and students practice the strategy together as the teacher begins to give students more responsibility for task engagement and completion. | |
| **Collaborative Practice**<br>In pairs and small groups, students work together on the strategy, sharing their thinking processes with one another, as the teacher checks in with each group. | |
| **Independent Practice**<br>Students practice the strategy on their own with regular feedback from other students and the teacher. | |
| **Time to Talk About Reading**<br>Students share their learning with one another. | |

"Gradual Release of Responsibility Note-Taking Grid" handout, available on Resources CD-ROM

As teachers are viewing the lesson, ask them to use the "Gradual Release of Responsibility Viewing Guide" (see the *Staff Development Resources* CD-ROM) as they take notes. The viewing guide asks them to notice teacher and student behaviors for each step of the gradual release as well as jot down any questions they have.

## Gradual Release of Responsibility Viewing Guide

| Segment | What do you notice about the teacher? | What do you notice about the students? | Lingering Questions and/or Comments … |
|---|---|---|---|
| **Setting the Stage:** Engage the Kids | | | |
| **Modeling:** Make Thinking Visible | | | |
| **Guided Practice:** Respond in Writing | | | |
| **Wrapping Up:** Share Thinking | | | |
| **Independent Practice:** Choose Text and Respond | | | |
| **Whole-Group Share** | | | |

"Gradual Release of Responsibility Viewing Guide" handout, , available on Resources CD-ROM

**Discuss the gradual release in action**   Following the demonstration lesson, reflect on each part of the gradual release by discussing teacher moves, teacher language, and student responses. During this discussion, highlight the essential language the teacher provides and how the goal of releasing the responsibility for thinking and reading to students was accomplished. Address any questions or concerns teachers may have, and wrap up with a review of each step of the framework. (Refer teachers to the summary of the GRR teaching steps in the *Toolkit* Teacher's Guides if necessary: *The Primary Comprehension Toolkit* Teacher's Guide, page 10, and/or *The Comprehension Toolkit* Teacher's Guide, page 24.)

# Session 2: Implementing Effective Conferences

"Conferring has more to do with learning how to listen than learning what to say" is a key message in Joanne Hindley's *In the Company of Children* (Stenhouse 1996). Conferring is at the heart of the gradual release of responsibility model. Sitting down next to a child and talking one-on-one with him or her give you a window into where the learner falls on the independence continuum. Is he ready for independence? Does she need additional support? The right questions and prompts can help you move that student toward greater independence and responsibility. We bring to the conference all we know about our kids as readers and people. We can't confer effectively with kids when we don't know them, so we spend time talking to kids about their interests, their lives, and their literate lives so we can begin to know them well enough to help them when we confer. And above all, we listen to them!

Conferring in the *Toolkits* occurs primarily during collaborative and independent practice. In this workshop, you will examine the conferences in the collaborative and independent practice sections from one of the strategy books together and then select and analyze other *Toolkit* conferences, making note of what makes an effective conference. Finally, you will have them select, read, and discuss "Conferring Considerations" and determine their own priorities for implementing conferring in their classrooms.

## Purpose
To observe and reflect on effective conferences in the *Toolkit* model

## Materials
*For each participant:*
- Copy of *The Primary Toolkit*, Lesson 16, pages 8–9
- Copy of the "Conferring Considerations" handout (see the *Staff Development Resources* CD-ROM)

*Ask teachers to bring:*
- Several strategy books from their own *Toolkits*

*For the coach:*
- List titled "Suggested Conferences to Analyze"

## *Workshop Steps*

**Share workshop goals**    Explain to participants that part of an effective gradual release of responsibility model is constant monitoring of students' readiness to be released. Brief conferences with one or two children, which they will be looking at in this session, are a key element in ensuring that release is gradual—or rapid—enough for each student. By the end of the session, the goal is to come to a shared vision of what makes effective conferring.

**Examine a *Toolkit* conference**    Distribute copies of pages 8 and 9 from the *Determine Importance* strategy book in *The Primary Comprehension Toolkit*. Ask teachers to read the three conferences in the "Collaborate" section. Point out that the conferences are with pairs of students. Suggest that they notice the following:

- Language used to engage kids in the conference. What questions were asked to prompt their thinking?
- Purpose of the conference. Is the purpose to support children's use of determining important strategies, understanding content, or both?
- Children's responses. What do the children's responses tell you about their grasp of ideas? Of determining importance?
- Different lengths of the conferences. How long does each one take?
- Ways the conferences supported gradual release. How did each one help children understand the text, concept, strategy, or content?

**Analyze additional *Toolkit* conferences**    The *Toolkit* lessons model the same kind of language throughout the "Guided Practice"—whether collaborative or independent—sections. Have teachers pair off to study additional conference examples. Display the following list of suggested lessons, and propose that partners scan the practice sections, looking at how both the teaching moves and the teaching language further the kids' thinking.

**The Primary Comprehension Toolkit**
*Activate and Connect*, Lesson 5, pages 19–20
*Activate and Connect*, Lesson 6, page 36
*Ask Questions*, Lesson 10, page 40
*Infer and Visualize*, Lesson 13, page 37
*Summarize and Synthesize*, Lesson 21, page 38

**The Comprehension Toolkit**
*Monitor Comprehension*, Lesson 3, pages 30–31
*Ask Questions*, Lesson 8, pages 19–20

*Infer Meaning*, Lesson 11, pages 20–21
*Determine Importance*, Lesson 17, pages 18–19
*Summarize and Synthesize*, Lesson 22, pages 7–9

After teachers have had ample time to read and discuss examples in their pairs, ask them to share out. What elements of language and teaching moves did they notice?

**Discuss effective conferences**

Distribute and discuss "Conferring Considerations," explaining that these provide big-picture principles to guide conferences. Remind teachers to think about the *Toolkit* conferences they just discussed, and solicit additional

---

### Conferring Considerations
page 1 of 2

- **Know your kids as readers.** There is much to talk about and recommend when we know our kids' reading interests, passions, and curiosities. We can recommend a constellation of reading possibilities for them when we know them as readers, and we can only make a difference in their learning if we know them well.

- **Use conferences to build rapport.** We can build rapport with our kids when we confer with them. Teaching is all about relationships. One-on-one conferences provide a great vehicle for building rapport.

- **"Teach the reader, not the reading."** The quote from Don Graves reminds us to focus on the reader, not just on a particular text at hand. In that way, we give our readers tools to work with as they read independently in a variety of texts.

- **"Celebrate and Extend."** Shelley Harwayne reminds us that as we confer with children, we should find something to celebrate about the reading, something they did well, what their engagement level is, and so on. Then we should choose something they can work on to extend their thinking so they have something to consider after we leave.

- **"How's it going?"** Carl Anderson uses this as a great icebreaker when conferring. Many kids let us know; others are less inclined to share. But start out this way and see what happens. Hoist the flag and see who salutes!

- **"Nothing matters more than your thinking."** We educators need to be insatiably curious about kids' thinking. Conferences show our interest implicitly, but don't forget to tell them explicitly every now and then!

- **Listen carefully and follow kids' lead.** Conferences are a great place to really listen to our kids and hear their needs. Only then can we teach them.

- **Be alert to discovery.** When we listen to our kids in conferences, we discover more about them as readers and more about ourselves as teachers. This discovery can fuel further learning and teaching for both students and teachers.

**Conferring Considerations** page 2 of 2

- **Expect the unexpected.** We often come to conferences with preconceived notions. If we are prepared for the unexpected, whatever it may be, we won't be totally stymied when we hear something surprising.

- **Use conferences to inform future instruction.** Individual conferences can tell us where to go next with a particular child and even sometimes where to go next with the whole class.

- **Teach explicitly in conferences.** Kids learn by watching and doing, not by watching and being told what to do. We should model our thinking in a conference the same way that we model our thinking in a minilesson. Often we use our minilessons for modeling thinking but then only tell kids what to do in our conferences. We should think aloud and model our thinking in minilessons, in small groups, and in conferences.

- **Share your own reading process.** It is always helpful to share our own reading process with readers, in conferences as well as in groups, so they can watch and hear about our literate lives— our struggles as well as our successes.

- **Link the conference to the lesson.** We should link instruction to practice, noticing if readers are using a strategy or skill gleaned from recent minilessons. If so, we should celebrate that as something good readers do. If not, we can explicitly make that link for them and encourage them to practice minilesson content in their reading.

- **Leave students with a goal.** We can help the readers think of a plan for their further reading so they can practice something in their independent reading that will develop proficiency.

- **Record the conference's key points.** We should keep written records of conferences, jotting down what we taught, what we learned, and what the reader's general disposition toward reading was at the time of the conference.

- **Check back in.** We need to touch base with the students again in relation to the conferences. We can also read their responses, listen to their conversations, and watch them to assess our next instructional moves.

"Conferring Considerations" handout, available on the Resources CD-ROM

thoughts and ideas to add to the list. Write these on a chart to consider as you plan your next steps.

**Determine next steps**    Either as a group or as individuals, decide on specific aspects of conferring to concentrate on in the coming weeks. Your plans could be as simple as trying out Carl Anderson's "How's it going?" or as ambitious as implementing a prescribed number of conferences each day—and keeping records of them. Arrange to be available to teachers in their classrooms to observe, coach, or demonstrate, and let them know you'll be around.

# Ongoing Support

### Study Groups

- **Lesson planning.** As your teachers begin to use the *Toolkits*, they may find that they would like to use a text in addition to or instead of the text provided in the *Toolkits*. Organizing collaborative lesson planning is one way you can help them be sure to incorporate the steps of the GRR model as well as the essential teaching language and moves into their instruction. As you are working with teachers to plan, begin by looking at the *Toolkit* lesson and discussing the strategy and the goals of the lesson. Using the Lesson Guide language and the "Gradual Release of Responsibility Lesson Planning" sheet (see the *Staff Development Resources* CD-ROM), work with your teachers to plan for each portion of the lesson, referring to the Lesson Guide for support with language and teaching moves.

- **Beginnings of gradual release.** Make copies of Linda Fielding and P. David Pearson's seminal research article on the gradual release of responsibility ("Reading Comprehension: What Works?" *Educational Leadership* 51,5: 62–67), and share them with your study group members. (See the *Staff Development Resources* CD-ROM.) Discuss how the authors' notions have morphed, have expanded, and have been applied in the decades since they first proposed them in 1994.

- **Book groups.** Read *Conferring with Readers: Supporting Each Student's Growth and Independence*, by Jennifer Serravallo and Gravity Goldberg (Heinemann, 2007). Based on the premise that a great reading conference only takes five minutes but can put a student on the path to becoming a better, more independent reader, the book outlines a supportive conference framework, provides explicit teaching methods for effective reading conferences, and suggests ideas for record keeping.

- **Development of conference protocol.** If your school does not already have a reading conference form, a study group might decide on a basic procedure for conferences and develop a form to both prompt their conferences and keep track of what they learn about each child. The "Conferring Considerations" handout in this lesson and the Serravallo and Goldberg book referenced in the paragraph on book groups can provide grist for the group's planning. If the group needs further inspiration, share the "Independent Reading Conference Form" on the *Staff Development Resources* CD-ROM.

## *In-Class Coaching*

- **When teachers could use help with their teaching structure,** charting a teaching sequence alongside the gradual release of responsibility framework might help make areas needing improvement clear. Use a copy of the "Gradual Release of Responsibility Note-Taking Grid" while you observe a lesson, noting in the right-hand column what the teacher is doing along the gradual release sequence. (You may have to number the teaching steps in the order they happen if the teacher's approach doesn't match the GRR sequence, and you may need the back of the page to note elements that do not appear in the GRR framework at all.) In a post-conference, review your notes with the teacher, and brainstorm other ways the lesson might be taught.

- **When teachers are already comfortable with the GRR framework,** work with them on applying it to other subject areas beyond literacy. Observe a math or science lesson, taking notes on which parts of the GRR model the teacher used. In the debrief, brainstorm ways the teacher could either strengthen the lesson by reinstating "missing" parts of the GRR framework or liven up one or more of the steps if the whole GRR framework is there.

- **When you need to provide support with conferring** (and everyone, even the most experienced conferrer, could profit from additional work on this), spend time in the classroom conferring yourself—as a demonstration for the teacher or as experience for students in the process—or observing the teacher as he or she confers, taking notes and later debriefing. If you have convened a study group to formalize the process (see the suggested study groups in this chapter), use the forms and process you have developed to guide and track teachers' conferences.

# Frequently Asked Questions

**What if I don't have the time in my schedule to complete an entire *Toolkit* lesson in one day? Where/how should I break it up?**

This question comes up often, and the answer hinges on the GRR model. If you have to break up a *Toolkit* lesson into two days, include the connecting and engaging, modeling, and guided practice portions of the *Toolkit* lesson on day one. On day two, model briefly for a moment or two to refresh the kids' memories about the lesson the day before, and then send them off for collaborative practice and/or independent practice followed by a sharing session. It is very important that students (especially less developed readers) have the opportunity to *immediately* practice the strategy with support from the teacher or fellow students after explicit instruction; this is the purpose of guided practice. If teachers end a lesson by modeling without guided practice, they run the risk that many of the students will not internalize the strategy.

5

**I was working with the staff** of a brand-new school whose principal believed in the higher-order thinking and gradual release of responsibility imbedded in the *Toolkit* lessons. She asked me to work with her staff, kindergarten through fifth grade, modeling and observing implementation of both the primary and intermediate *Toolkits*. Depending on their experience and comfort with the *Toolkits*, as well as their students' needs, teachers were at varying stages of implementation. During one visit, I observed a fifth grade teacher introducing the strategy of determining importance (Lesson 16) and a first grade teacher introducing creating mental images (Lesson 13) with a text she chose on her own. The teachers were different, the children were different, the lessons were different, but the coaching for both teachers was similar: both needed support in modeling how a proficient reader thinks through a text. They both told their students what to do, but they never explicitly thought aloud or demonstrated **how** to do it.

Each of the *Toolkit* lessons the teachers were using included the Model step. But it wasn't explicit in their teaching. My post-lesson conferences for each of the teachers began the same way: "It was clear to me what you wanted your students to do because you told them and you had your focus written on the board. But what did you notice about your students?"

The answers from the teachers were similar. "Well, I think some of them struggled with the idea. They didn't seem to get it like I hoped they would." As the conferences continued, I shared with both teachers that students' chances of success with any lesson are greater when modeling is provided. Interestingly enough, both teachers thought they **had** modeled the strategy. But when we reviewed the language they used in the lesson, they realized they hadn't really modeled; rather, they had talked about the strategy, the task, and the text. They had not modeled how they as proficient readers construct meaning. This is not surprising. We often do what's been done to us. Few of us had the opportunity to watch our teachers open up their own reading process by thinking aloud in front of us. When teachers peel back the layers of their own reading and thinking process, they are actually engaging in an apprentice model of literacy learning. Just as the young blacksmith watches the master blacksmith shoeing horses, our kids can watch adult readers creating meaning and experiencing what happens for readers as they read, and our students can see how adult readers struggle through hurdles as well as find joy in words and are stimulated and energized by issues and ideas.

To close this coaching session, I picked up the texts and showed both of these teachers what I was thinking as I read them. I suggested they too might want to think about how they constructed meaning as they read. Before closing, we reviewed the language used in the In Action and Lesson Guide portions of the lessons and planned how to revisit the strategy during the next day's lesson. I also suggested that they might try to consciously think about their personal reading process in their own reading life over the next few days. As proficient adult readers, we automatically create meaning when we read, but this automaticity can interfere with our conscious thinking about our own reading. So it is a good idea to think about our own process to share with our teachers and their kids.

The *Toolkits* provide the focus, language, and teaching moves for each lesson, but teachers may still need support with implementation of the lessons. Although the *Toolkits* provide explicit language and teaching moves for the gradual release framework, teachers won't always teach the lesson exactly as it was written. That's expected. The lesson moves and lesson language are merely suggestions to guide teachers as they implement *Toolkit* instruction. The lessons were never intended to be scripts. But for maximum effectiveness, we hope teachers will embrace the methods in each lesson part. We encourage teachers to use every lesson part and study the Lesson Guide for the essential language necessary to model the strategy for students. We can support this by pre-planning with teachers—talking through the teaching moves, planning the language for the lesson, and exploring how we think when we read so we can model that for our kids. Your coaching will allow teachers to reflect and fine-tune their instruction as they become more comfortable with the teaching moves and strategies included in the *Toolkits*.

# Introduction

## Think-Alouds and Demonstrations: What, Why, and When

You'll notice that in the *Toolkit* lessons, a running instructional narrative—interspersed with frequent opportunities for student participation—dominates the In Action section. This teacher talk is the vehicle for guiding the thinking about and responding to texts and ideas. Within this lesson development, the modeling step is the core of strategy instruction. Modeling provides the opportunity to show kids, not just tell them, what the strategy looks like in action. Two teaching methods are critical to modeling: think-alouds and demonstrations.

### What Are Think-Alouds and Demonstrations?

During the modeling portion of each lesson, teachers are thinking aloud and demonstrating for students how to do the specified strategy. For example, if the lesson focus is determining importance, teachers model *how* to determine which details are important out of all the details that are there. This requires the teacher to do two things that are connected but not exactly the same: *thinking aloud* and *demonstrating*. When thinking aloud, teachers orally walk the students through the reading and thinking that they, as proficient readers, go through to use the strategy—in this instance, walking students through finding the details that are important and thinking aloud about how you knew the details were important. *Demonstrating* can be thought of as using physical objects (charts, Post-its, thinksheets) and actions (underlining, highlighting, writing notes in the margin, connecting with arrows, coding text, and so on) to show thinking. In effective instruction, think-alouds and demonstrations go hand in hand. Both teaching methods are necessary.

### When Do Teachers Need Coaching in Think-Alouds and Demonstrations?

The concept of using think-alouds and demonstrations to model the thinking process may be new to many teachers. As mentioned earlier, many of us never had teachers who shared their thinking and demonstrated how they construct meaning. As you visit classrooms, you may see teachers providing instruction by *telling* rather than *showing*. Their explanations and their assignments may be focused and clear, but if they don't walk students through the process by modeling thinking, demonstrating, and giving kids time to practice, the results will likely be less than they hoped for. As you work with teachers, look closely together at the Model section of the *Toolkit* lesson. Discuss how the explicit teaching language and demonstrations support kids to access the strategy. And keep in mind that the foundation of this method—thinking through what you do as a reader and articulating those processes so students understand—can be challenging. Think-alouds require teachers to think through a process that is automatic for them, and this can be difficult. Planning for think-alouds will take practice, and it offers a perfect opportunity to work collaboratively with grade levels or groups of teachers to think through and plan instruction with the same text together. Multiple workshops, study-group sessions, and in-class coaching can provide opportunities for teachers to become more skilled at thinking aloud and demonstrating for their students.

The following workshops and suggestions for ongoing coaching, support, and follow-up provide several different options for thinking through the language and teaching moves that make for purposeful modeling sessions.

# Workshop

## Session 1: Exploring Effective Think-Alouds and Demonstrations

Modeling is an essential step in the Gradual Release of Responsibility framework and merits particular attention and support. This session includes:

- Introducing modeling—distinguishing between think-alouds and demonstrations
- Establishing criteria for effective think-alouds and demonstrations
- Analyzing the think-alouds in a *Toolkit* lesson in groups using the criteria developed
- Identifying steps in creating think-alouds and demonstrations, and using gradual release to create think-alouds with new texts
- Sharing and critiquing each other's work

### Purpose

To explore the purpose and characteristics of effective think-alouds and demonstrations

### Materials

Preferably use the same text for all participants, but in a mixed group of primary and intermediate teachers, a lesson from both *Toolkits* may be included.

*Ask teachers to bring:*

- Lesson 12 from strategy book 4 (primary: *Infer & Visualize* strategy book, Lesson 12, "Infer Meaning," or intermediate: *Infer Meaning* strategy book, Lesson 12, "Tackle the Meaning of Language")
- *Toolkit* Teacher's Guide (either primary or intermediate)

*For the coach:*

- Chart paper for recording the Criteria for Think-Alouds and Demonstrations chart
- Markers

## Workshop Steps

**Share the goals and explain the terms *think-aloud* and *demonstration***

Explain that in this workshop, teachers will be working with two essential components of the modeling phase of the gradual release of responsibility—thinking aloud and demonstrating how to use the specified strategy. This workshop highlights how each contributes to thoughtful instruction. In effective instruction, think-alouds and demonstrations go hand in hand.

Explain that while *thinking aloud*, they, as proficient readers, orally walk their students through the reading and thinking that students, as proficient readers, go through to use the strategy. Let them know that thinking aloud makes thinking audible. *Demonstrating* is using physical objects (for example, charts, Post-its, thinksheets) or actions (underlining, highlighting, writing notes in the margin, connecting with arrows, coding text, and so on). Note that demonstrating makes thinking visible. Refer back to the section on think-alouds in the *Toolkit* Teacher's Guides (primary *Toolkit*, page 25; intermediate *Toolkit*, pages 13–14) for further explanation.

**Discuss the use of modeling in *Toolkit* lessons**

Ask participants to turn and talk about why modeling—both thinking aloud and demonstrating—are central to an effective *Toolkit* lesson. Discuss their responses. Emphasize that both teaching methods are necessary. A lesson including only demonstrations can leave a reader understanding the operation but not the underlying strategy. For example, you can demonstrate for students how to underline important information, but if you don't think aloud about how you decided which phrases were most important to underline, all students may learn is to underline with no strategy for figuring out what is important. Conversely, a think-aloud with no demonstration leaves you with no "thinking tracks"—and no way to tell if and how students are applying the strategy. These tracks enable teachers to examine and assess student progress and to plan future instruction. They also serve as visual maps for the students during modeling and guided practice, reinforcing kids' thinking. Learners will more closely notice and explore their own cognition by jotting it down.

As teachers plan think-alouds for strategy instruction, they will likely have a focus strategy for a particular lesson. For example, if the focus strategy is determining importance, teachers would sort and sift details to arrive at the most important ideas. However, kids will likely be questioning, connecting, inferring, and so on as they are thinking and reading. We honor all the strategic processes as well, even as we focus on a specific strategy.

**Chart the criteria**   Have teachers turn and talk about the criteria for think-alouds and demonstrations. Discuss and list their responses on a chart titled Criteria for Think-Alouds and Demonstrations. List criteria in the teachers' own words, and expect them to come up with others in addition to those listed here. Here's a list we brainstormed, but your list may be different.

**The teacher:**

- Shows his or her own thinking as she or he reads aloud a portion of the text.

- Includes in the think-aloud both the end result (e.g., question, inference) and the process of arriving at it.

- Keeps in mind the background knowledge, vocabulary, interests, strengths, and needs of the students.

- Uses clear language that is conversational and authentic.

- Shows how the focus strategy helps to understand the text.

- Emphasizes the focus strategy but models other strategies as they are needed for actually thinking through the text.

- Selects text points for modeling that are purposeful and contribute to making sense of what's important in the text.

- Leaves tracks of thinking visibly (using Post-its, writing in margins, etc.).

- Keeps kids engaged through turn and talk.

- Paces the think-aloud so that it is quick and to the point but sufficient for students to see the strategy in action.

- Writes enough to make the point but doesn't get bogged down.

**Analyze *Toolkit* think-alouds and demonstrations**   Using *Toolkit* Lesson 12 from strategy book 4, invite participants to read the Connect & Engage and Model portions of the lessons, paying particular attention to the think-alouds and demonstrations.

Ask participants to identify the first think-aloud and then in groups analyze it in relation to the criteria on the chart: *How does the think-aloud reflect the criteria?* Then have teachers share their observations. An example is given below for the think-aloud that begins in the modeling portion of the intermediate *Toolkit*'s Lesson 12 ("Infer Meaning," pages 28–29). Continue to have participants identify and analyze additional think-alouds in the lesson. You may want to jigsaw the think-alouds or choose a few that illustrate the criteria particularly clearly and stimulate discussion.

| Criteria for Think-Alouds/Demonstrations | Evidence |
|---|---|
| Shows his/her own thinking as she/he reads aloud a portion of the text | He/she asks the specific question, "Remembers what? What does the moon remember?" |
| Includes in the think-aloud both the end result (e.g., question, inference) and process of arriving at it | In addition to the question asked, he/she explains "I immediately asked a question; don't have an answer right now . . . ."<br><br>Then he/she goes on to infer the meaning of "marooned" using background knowledge. |
| Keeps in mind the background knowledge, vocabulary, interests, strengths, and needs of the students | It seems like most students would have the same question—helps them connect. |
| Uses clear language that is conversational and authentic | "Hmm, I wondered, since I don't have an answer right now." |

Ask teachers to share insights on think-alouds and demonstrations.

# Session 2: Creating Think-Alouds

As explained in the primary *Toolkit*'s Teacher's Guide (page 37), the lesson "In Action" is a snapshot of the teaching and learning in one classroom at a particular time; it is not a script. Therefore, this session will focus on supporting teachers to create their own think-alouds, with either the texts from the *Toolkit* lessons or texts of their choice.

## Purpose
To plan and create their own think-alouds

## Materials
*For each participant:*
- Copy of the poem "Secrets" (intermediate *Toolkit*, *Source Book of Short Text*, page 37) or another text of your choice

*Ask teachers to bring:*
- Lesson 12 Lesson Guide from strategy book 4 (primary: *Infer & Visualize*, Lesson 12, "Infer Meaning," pages 16–17; intermediate: *Infer Meaning*, Lesson 12, "Tackle the Meaning of Language," pages 34–35)
- Copy of text they will be using to create think-alouds

*For the coach:*

- Copy of the Criteria for Think-Alouds and Demonstrations chart created in the last session
- Anchor chart or handout of "Steps for Creating a Think-Aloud"

## Workshop Steps

**Review criteria established for effective think-alouds**

Display the Criteria for Think-Alouds and Demonstrations chart created in the last session. If time has elapsed since the previous session, participants could talk in groups about if and how the criteria have informed their thinking and practice with modeling since the last session. Encourage them to share out with the whole group.

Explain to participants that today they will be working in groups using the criteria to create their own think-alouds.

**Share steps taken to create a think-aloud**

Post the steps on a chart and/or distribute a sheet to participants.

### Steps for Creating a Think-Aloud

- Read the entire text.
- Think about the most important ideas in the text and what you want the students to understand from it.
- Think about how your focus strategy, in combination with other strategies or aspects of the inner conversation, will support developing that understanding.
- Consider your students—their background knowledge, vocabulary, interests, and needs.
- Consider the specific points in the text where you will stop and think out loud.
- Practice and jot down the words you will use to share your thinking each time you stop. Refine and revise as you think your way through the text.

**Give an example of starting to create a think-aloud**

Display or distribute copies of the poem "Secrets" from Lesson 12 in the intermediate *Toolkit*, or another choice of text, and think aloud your process: *"When I read this poem, I'm thinking that the poet is talking about how enormous space is and how many mysteries it has. The poet makes me realize that we have so many unanswered questions about space, and we don't know if we will ever have answers to them. But there is something compelling about all these mysteries of space, and our curiosity drives us to keep asking the questions. So now I'll go back and chunk the text to show the kids how my thinking develops as I think about specific words and phrases that lead me to infer these ideas. I will include other strategies as I authentically think my way through the poem. So I might start with a question, 'What does the poet mean by "Space keeps its secrets hidden/It does not tell."? What secrets is she talking about?' Then I read the next seven lines of the poem. Now I know from my background knowledge that these are a lot of questions that people have about space that we don't know answers to yet. So I'm inferring that these are the secrets that space keeps hidden."*

**Ask participants to think through the remainder of the text**

Have participants decide where they would stop to share their inner conversation, what they would say, and why. Then share think-alouds and use the criteria for effective think-alouds to reflect on the strengths of the think-alouds and ways to improve them. Discuss where you might include turn and talk and what demonstrations you would use to leave tracks of thinking.

**Have participants create and reflect on think-alouds**

Ask participants to work in groups to create their own think-alouds using the texts they brought. Support and share out.

**Reflect on think-alouds and demonstrations**

End this workshop by reflecting on think-alouds and demonstrations. Ask teachers to think through the last two sessions. How has their thinking about modeling changed or developed? If participants are keeping a journal of their teaching practices, encourage them to write their reflections down. Share.

# Ongoing Support

### *Study Groups*

- **Planning think-alouds.** Teachers can use the criteria for effective think-alouds and the steps for creating them to collaboratively develop think-alouds and demonstrations for their upcoming lessons. Some common pitfalls can be addressed:
  - **Explaining instead of sharing thinking.** "The phrase 'Space keeps its secrets hidden' means that human beings still have many unanswered questions about space."
  - **Reciting questions instead of sharing thinking.** "What does the phrase 'Space keeps its secrets hidden' mean?"
  - **Losing track of the focus on the strategy for understanding.** "What literary device does the poet use in the first stanza of 'Secrets'?"

- **Thinking about differentiation.** Pay special attention to the learning needs of English language learners (ELLs) and/or developing readers and writers in your classroom. *How might a think aloud/demonstration look different depending on the makeup of the class? What might children who need more support require?* Responses may include needing more visuals and pictures to make content comprehensible and to demonstrate thinking for ELLs; spend more time on the Connect & Engage portion of the lesson to build children's background knowledge and vocabulary on the lesson topic before launching into the modeling portion of the lesson. A *Toolkit* component, *Scaffolding Lessons for English Language Learners*, helps teachers support ELLs by providing a preview and a language extension for every *Toolkit* lesson. Another *Toolkit* component, *Comprehension Intervention*, breaks down the *Toolkit* lessons into additional small-group sessions to support developing readers to better use the *Toolkit* lessons to support comprehension. Both resources are available through www.heinemann.com and www.comprehensiontoolkit.com.

- **Doing ongoing reading and study.** Read and discuss the now-classic 1983 article on thinking aloud by Beth Davey titled "Think Aloud: Modeling the Cognitive Processes of Reading Comprehension" (*Journal of Reading* 27:44–47). (See the *Staff Development Resources* CD-ROM.)

## *In-Class Coaching*

■ **When you are reviewing teachers' demonstration lessons,** use notes from a lesson observation and ask teachers to reflect on the think-aloud/demonstration portion of the lesson. They might consider the following:

- Content of think-alouds—How did they meet the criteria?
- Delivery of think-alouds—Did the students remain engaged?
- Effect of the demonstrations—Did student work samples reflect the type of thinking modeled?
- Next steps—What will you build on and what will you change in modeling future lessons?

■ **When teachers are confident with respect to think-alouds and demonstrations,** encourage them to continue using new texts and to observe the results. Brainstorm additional demonstrations to vary the teaching approach; consider how think-alouds and demonstrations change as students become more proficient with specific strategies over time. Remind teachers that the lesson guide is a powerful scaffold for think-alouds and demonstrations.

■ **When teachers are hesitant to try think-alouds and demonstrations,** sit down and plan an upcoming lesson together, using the steps and criteria outlined in the above workshops. It can be useful to "unpack" the process of thinking aloud and "showing, not telling" because this is a clear paradigm shift from instruction that focuses on explanation or recitation. At first, lead the process yourself, modeling what the think-aloud might look like. Gradually turn the process over to the teachers as planning proceeds. Depending on the planning, you can teach, co-teach, or observe the teachers teach the lesson. Co-teaching is a powerful way to share the responsibility for the lesson and support teachers to experience teaching the lesson but with added support. And once again, point out the lesson guides.

# Frequently Asked Questions

## How do I know how much to model?

We don't model any more than we absolutely have to. We keep our think-alouds short and sweet. We engage kids quickly in having a go at it. See Chapter 4, "Not So Gradual Release," by Debbie Miller, from *Comprehension Going Forward*. However, explicit think-alouds are definitely necessary when introducing a strategy for the first time or when working through a tough strategy or text. Students need to hear how their teacher and classmates work through a text using the focus strategy and may need several examples of thinking aloud before they understand what to do themselves. As a strategy becomes more familiar to the students, they may need less modeling. However, as the complexity of the text increases, thinking aloud increases in importance.

We include turn and talk in the modeling so we can listen to kids and determine if they need additional modeling or are ready for guided or even independent practice. Our goal is to promote independence and to increase the proportion of time students apply strategies in their independent reading.

## Should kids write during the modeling?

It's generally easier to keep students' attention focused on what you are showing if they are not writing while you model. Also, it's unnecessary and not productive to have students copy everything you write, which is what may happen if they are writing during modeling. However, there is no hard-and-fast rule. There may be times when it is helpful for kids to focus on their thinking if they can listen and jot at the same time. They begin to do this as they get more comfortable with leaving tracks of their thinking. The line between modeling and guiding becomes less distinct.

## Should I let the students share their own thinking during the modeling?

Students mainly share their thinking through turning and talking. This helps the teacher keep the modeling short and focused. It takes considerable skill to include student comments in the modeling and not get

## Frequently Asked Questions (continued)

sidetracked or muddy the clear examples you are trying to provide. But model quickly for a minute or two, and then have kids turn and talk to process the information. Let a few share and then model again for several minutes. Finally, have students process through discussion. Modeling thinking is not a linear process but rather a recursive and dynamic one.

**I've trained numerous teachers** to implement *The Comprehension Toolkit*. I've worked with teachers from high-socioeconomic schools where the majority of kids come from homes that are filled with books and where many of them start school already reading. I've also worked in high-poverty schools where many of the students have limited access to books and enter school without letter recognition. But regardless of where teachers teach, by the time we're halfway through the *Toolkit* training, they all recognize the importance of comprehension strategies and are eager to learn more about the *Toolkits*. And by the time we get to the end of the Toolkit training, they all ask the same question: "How do I get grades from this?"

The answer isn't a simple one, and I usually begin my answer with the difference between assessment and evaluation: "**Assessment** guides your instruction by showing you what students can and can't do. **Evaluation** places a judgment, a value, or a grade on the work students produce. It's an end result." The *Toolkit* assessment opportunities in every lesson provide insight into students' thinking and abilities. This assessment allows you to plan for tomorrow's instruction and is very useful.

But for most of us, grades are a reality. So many teachers using the *Toolkits* rely on a tried-and-true method that has lasted through decades of education reform—the very reliable √, √+, and √−. These provide you with the evaluation, or grade, you want, but when they are used correctly—to determine which students need additional support and which students just need more practice on their own in texts they can read—they can also help to guide your instruction. Most likely you'll be able to divide the work students produce into three groups and differentiate instruction accordingly: providing further teaching and support for kids who didn't get it (√−), creating opportunities for further practice for kids who got it but may not have mastered it (√), and encouraging practice in challenging texts or a new genre for those who nailed it (√+).

I know this isn't the answer that most teachers expect or want, so I ask a few questions: "How do you put a letter grade or percentage on a mental image or a question a student had while reading? If students are reading *Charlotte's Web* and one pictures a fading red barn and another pictures a brown barn, does one receive an A or a 90 percent and another receive a C or a 72 percent?" When we consider a grade in this example, it can seem a bit ridiculous. So the long-winded answer to the question "How do I get grades from this?" is best answered by figuring out three things: (1) What do we know about our students as readers? (2) What do we need to teach them in order for them to become better readers? (3) How will we know they've made progress toward becoming better readers? When those three questions are answered, finding out how to gather grades will become more clear.

# Introduction

## Assessment and Evaluation: What, Why, and When

Assessment, evaluation, and grades are a real part of schools' and teachers' lives. While everyone has their own belief system about these things, the *most* important thing to remember is to be fair to students. To quote *The Comprehension Toolkit* Teacher's Guide, "Evaluation [grading] is about putting a value on the work. We evaluate only after students have had time to practice a new strategy or skill. We don't grade what kids already know: we grade what they have learned with practice. When we evaluate, we make sure the grades are based on evidence gleaned from ongoing and authentic assessment" (page 43).

### What Are Assessment and Evaluation?

As noted in the beginning of this chapter, *assessment* guides instruction by demonstrating what a student can or cannot do. *Evaluation* judges the student's work, placing a value or a grade on it. When **assessing** students' performance on comprehension strategies, teachers consider the following:

1. Are students using the strategy to gain understanding?
2. What kinds of thinking—connections, insights, inferences, and so on—are they using?
3. How are they using their thinking to respond to the topic or text and make meaning from it?

When **evaluating** students' performance on comprehension strategies, teachers consider the following:

1. Where did students start in relation to the strategy being taught?
2. How long have they had to practice?
3. What kind of support was provided?

When teachers are reporting progress or grades to parents or their administrators, the answers to these questions need to be discussed in addition to the grade. What we are all after is student learning and progress; grades are a by-product of this goal, not the end result. The more we discuss these ideas, the more comfortable teachers will become with ways to talk about progress beyond a letter grade or percentage.

# Workshop

## Session 1: Differentiating Between Assessment and Evaluation

Because teachers often hold very strong opinions about assessment, evaluation, and grades, the initial coaching session revolves around discussing the difference between assessment and evaluation and explores the ongoing assessment opportunities and the annotated rubrics in the *Toolkits*. Session 2 then focuses on the purposes of evaluation, the effective products for evaluation, and the rubrics and master trackers designed to show progress over time.

**Note:** The workshop outlined here is based on Lesson 1, "Follow Your Inner Conversation," in strategy book 1, *Monitor Comprehension*, of *The Comprehension Toolkit*, but you can focus on any strategy to make the same points. If you have a group of primary teachers only, we suggest you use Lesson 8, "View and Read to Learn and Wonder," in the *Ask Questions* strategy book. If you have teachers from varying grade levels, explain that you will be using the intermediate *Monitor Comprehension* strategy book to explore assessment but that the assessment process is the same regardless of which *Toolkit* you are using.

Before conducting this workshop, teach the lesson (in this workshop, "Follow Your Inner Conversation") and collect student work. Make copies of the student work for all workshop participants. Because students use Post-its to reflect their thinking in this lesson, there may be many, many Post-its collected. For training purposes, you'll need only representative samples. You might collect 8 to 10 Post-its reflecting various types of answers—those showing strong evidence, some evidence, and little evidence of strategy use. Place these Post-its randomly on two sheets of paper. (Don't categorize them; leave that to the teachers.) Next, make a copy for each participant plus a few extras for those who might have forgotten to bring their copies to the second session. Alternatively—and ideally—enlist a teacher to gather work samples from every lesson in a strategy book from a handful of students. Use the Lesson 1 Post-its in this session and the rest of the work samples in Session 2 or in study groups on this topic.

## Purpose

To define assessment and evaluation and study what the *Toolkit* offers to support assessment

## Materials

*For each participant:*

- Copy of Lesson 1, "Follow Your Inner Conversation," in strategy book 1, *Monitor Comprehension* (intermediate *Toolkit*)
- Copy of *How Many Days to America?* (intermediate *Toolkit* Trade Book Pack)
- Copy of student work for Lesson 1, "Follow Your Inner Conversation," in strategy book 1, *Monitor Comprehension* (intermediate *Toolkit*)
- Copy of "Annotated Rubric for Strategy Cluster 1: Monitor Comprehension" on page 40 from strategy book 1, *Monitor Comprehension* (intermediate *Toolkit*)

*Ask teachers to bring:*

- *Toolkit* Teacher's Guide (either primary or intermediate)

*For the coach:*

- Anchor chart with two columns labeled "Assessment" and "Evaluation"
- Document camera or an interactive whiteboard to project student work

## *Workshop Steps*

**Define *assessment* and *evaluation* and share workshop goals**

Begin this session by asking teachers to think for a moment about assessment and evaluation and grades. Discuss the two terms and the difference between them: *assessment* uses student work as evidence to show what the learner can or cannot do, and its end result is differentiated instruction; *evaluation* uses student work as evidence of relative mastery, and its end result is a grade.

Explain to participants that during this workshop, we will be discussing both assessment and evaluation (grading), concentrating on assessment in the first session and evaluation in the second, and encourage them to take notes about new ideas or useful practices they might incorporate into their day-to-day instruction.

**Discuss assessment and evaluation**

Ask participants to read the *Toolkit* Teacher's Guide's section on assessment, stopping before the section on rubrics (*The Primary Toolkit* Teacher's Guide, pages 56–58; *The Comprehension Toolki*t Teacher's Guide, pages 43–44) and taking notes about the points they feel are most important. Provide time for participants to turn and talk about what they've read, and then open up a group discussion. Ask for a few volunteers to share out what they felt was important to remember about assessment and why.

**Chart the similarities and differences between assessment and evaluation**

As teachers share out, record their ideas in the appropriate column of the Assessment and Evaluation anchor chart. List the attributes that assessment and evaluation have in common (e.g., based on evidence: student work) in both columns, and describe attributes that are different (e.g., purpose, timing) in their respective columns. Build the understanding that assessment is ongoing and informs instruction whereas evaluation occurs at specific benchmark points and measures growth over time.

**Assessment and Evaluation**

| Assessment | Evaluation |
| --- | --- |
| | |

"Assessment and Evaluation" anchor chart

**Ensure familiarity with the lesson text**

If teachers are familiar with the lesson and *How Many Days to America?*, give them a brief reminder of what the book is about. If teachers are not familiar with the book, provide the gist of the lesson and either read aloud the story or ask them to read through the book with their tablemates. They will need to be familiar with the story in order to assess student responses.

**Note *Toolkit* lesson goals**

Give teachers a copy of Lesson 1, "Follow Your Inner Conversation," in strategy book 1, *Monitor Comprehension* (intermediate *Toolkit*). Ask teachers to turn and look at the "Goals & Assessment" (page 3) section as you read aloud the lesson goals. Discuss the fact that the lesson goals—what we want students to be able to do—are tightly linked with lesson assessment. The purpose of assessment is to gauge whether or not students meet these goals. Have them flip to "Reflection & Assessment" (page 9) at the end of the lesson and note that the assessment questions are mirror images of the goals.

**Walk through assessment models**

Then turn their attention to the exemplar Post-its and the *Toolkit*'s analysis. Walk them through the sample student work and captions, relating them to the lesson goals and the lesson text. Make sure to discuss the rationale of why the responses are labeled as they are and to entertain teachers' ideas of other conclusions to be drawn from the Post-its. Much can be learned about students' thinking from a few words on a Post-it!

**Guide assessment of student samples**

After you've gone through the exemplar texts together, pass out the student examples you collected during your lesson. Ask teachers to work in groups to determine which of the responses demonstrate understanding and which need clarification or intervention. Suggest that they categorize the responses in those two categories: (1) demonstrates understanding and (2) needs clarification or intervention. As teachers are working in groups, take the time to sit with the different groups as they work together. This will allow you to gain insight into their thinking and answer any lingering questions and will help you plan for the next session.

After teachers have had time to work together, discuss the responses aloud with the group. Ask teachers to share not only how they assessed the responses (demonstrates understanding or needs intervention and clarification) but why they placed them in that category.

**Revisit lesson goals and assessment in relation to the annotated rubric**

Give teachers the strategy-specific rubric titled "Annotated Rubric for Strategy Cluster 1: Monitor Comprehension" from the intermediate *Toolkit*'s strategy book 1, *Monitor Comprehension*. Explain to teachers that this is the annotated rubric referenced in the *Toolkit* Teacher's Guide, and remind them that this is a tool for documenting strategy use over time—cumulative evidence across the entire unit. Point out to participants that the rubric for each strategy includes opportunities to assess all lesson goals in this strategy book; have them mark this rubric from the intermediate *Toolkit* with a Post-it. Then turn to the "Goals & Assessment" section at the beginning of each lesson in the strategy book that they are using. Note the correspondence of the goals with the summary rubric.

Then focus attention on the "Reflection & Assessment" section of the lesson in each of the strategy books. The assessments will vary and may include Post-its, two-column forms, text annotations, etc. Student responses will also differ. Discuss why it is important to use a variety of different responses to assess student learning. Also talk about how children differ and demonstrate their understanding in different ways. As kids become more acquainted with *Toolkit* strategy instruction, they may favor one response option over another.

**Note how the annotated rubric reflects unit goals**

Once teachers have read through and discussed assessment across the strategy book, have them turn back to the annotated rubric. Note how the goals of each lesson appear on the annotated rubric. This rubric allows you, after students have had ample time to practice the strategy, to evaluate student performance. An important thing to remember is that assessment should always be considered in relation to planning for instruction.

When using the annotated rubric to evaluate student work, teachers should also consider how their instruction needs to change based on the needs of the students. The annotated rubric with student work samples attached allows you to see at a quick glance where students may need additional support and practice. Remind teachers that each of the strategy books contains an annotated rubric to help guide instruction and articulate student progress.

# Session 2: Implementing Effective Evaluation

This part of the workshop focuses on evaluation, grading students' work. Effective evaluation should measure progress demonstrating children's learning and understanding. Providing collaborative time to look at students' work at the beginning and at the end of a unit will help teachers evaluate student performance in terms of growth over time rather than passing or failing before students have had the opportunity to learn and practice. We never grade our students' work until we have modeled very explicitly with different texts and given students plenty of time to practice both collaboratively and independently. We want to grade what children have learned rather than what they knew or have not yet learned.

**Note:** The workshop outlined here is based on Lesson 5, "Merge Thinking with New Learning," in strategy book 2, *Activate & Connect*, of *The*

*Comprehension Toolkit*, but you can focus on any strategy to make the same points. If you have a group of primary teachers only, we suggest you use Lesson 7, "Merge Thinking with New Learning: Stop, Think, and React to Information," in the *Activate & Connect* strategy book. If you have teachers from varying grade levels, explain that you will be using the intermediate *Activate & Connect* strategy book to explore assessment but that the assessment process is the same regardless of which *Toolkit* you are using.

### Purpose

To review the definitions of assessment and evaluation and study what the *Toolkits* offer to support teachers in evaluation and grading

### Materials

*For each participant:*

- Copy of Lesson 5, "Merge Thinking with New Learning," in strategy book 2, *Activate & Connect* (intermediate *Toolkit*)
- Copy of "Annotated Rubric for Strategy Cluster 2: Activate and Connect" on page 40 in strategy book 2, *Activate & Connect* (intermediate *Toolkit*)

*Ask teachers to bring:*

- *Toolkit* Teacher's Guide (either primary or intermediate)

*For the coach:*

- Two-column anchor chart titled Assessment and Evaluation from Session 1 of this workshop
- Document camera for projecting student work

## *Workshop Steps*

**Share session goals and review terms**  Display the Assessment and Evaluation anchor chart created in the first session. Explain to participants that first they'll review the terms *assessment* and *evaluation* and then move into a focus on evaluation, reviewing two tools that the *Toolkit* provides for evaluation and devising evaluation methods of their own. To begin the session, remind teachers of the distinction between assessment and evaluation. Ask if any participants have had an opportunity to assess student responses, and have them share out among the group.

**Revisit the *Toolkit* philosophy on assessment and evaluation**

Ask participants to turn again to the assessment section in their *Toolkit* Teacher's Guide (*The Primary Toolkit*, pages 56–58; *The Comprehension Toolkit*, pages 43–46), this time concentrating on evaluation and the rubric.

Explain that the *Toolkits* take care to assess, but not evaluate, kids' raw thinking. It is important that students feel free to explore their thoughts, take risks, and not feel constrained by meeting the teacher's approval. We want their focus to be on learning—not on pleasing their teacher. But evaluation does serve certain purposes. Read aloud the statement on page 43 of *The Comprehension Toolkit*'s Teacher's Guide: "We evaluate students to hold them accountable for their learning, to grade their understanding, and to satisfy the norms of school and society."

**Point out the annotated rubrics**

Give teachers a copy of the strategy-specific rubric titled "Annotated Rubric for Strategy Cluster 2: Activate and Connect" on page 40 in the intermediate *Toolkit*'s strategy book 2, *Activate & Connect*. Explain that this is an evaluation tool for documenting strategy use over time—cumulative evidence across the entire unit. Have them note that the first evidence descriptor, "Understands the purpose of text and visual features," is a distillation of the lesson's goals and corresponds to the student work discussed in the last session.

**Review the *Toolkit* master trackers**

Talk about the blank master tracker forms at the back of the *Toolkit* Teacher's Guides (*The Primary Comprehension Toolkit*, pages 69–70; *The Comprehension Toolkit*, pages 45–46). In addition to individual strategy rubrics, the *Toolkits* also provide two Master Trackers: a Class Record and an Individual Record. The Class Record allows you to see at a glance how students are performing in relation to each of the strategies; list student names down the left-hand column, and keep anecdotal records about each strategy in the row next to each child's name. The Individual Record can be used alone or in conjunction with the Class Record and allows an at-a-glance look at one student's performance in relation to each of the strategies. This rubric in particular can be extremely helpful when articulating progress to parents and administrators.

**Discuss the purposes of evaluation**

Write the three purposes of evaluation—grading students' understanding, holding students accountable for their learning, and satisfying the norms of school and society—on a chart. As a whole group, discuss these purposes and ways they might meet them. Guide the discussion with the following principles behind each purpose:

■ **Grade students' understanding.** Make sure only to grade *products* of students' thinking, something they have developed to show their best work, rather than the Post-its or text coding that they do on the spot as they read. What products could do this?

■ **Hold kids accountable for their learning.** If you are spending the kind of time the *Toolkits* suggest teaching thinking strategies as tools for learning, kids ought to learn, understand, and remember content better than ever before and show that they have added to their knowledge over time. Assess content acquisition, not by testing students with low-level fill-in-the-blank or multiple-choice tests but rather by asking students to write or draw what they have learned and explaining why it matters. What ways could we evaluate their understanding over time?

■ **Satisfy norms of school and society.** Think about *other* products that can be given a grade in a reading class besides strategy application. What other ways could you satisfy the requirements for grades so you don't feel obligated to grade Post-its or raw thinking just to get grades?

**Brainstorm ways to satisfy the three purposes of evaluation**

Divide participants into three groups, and ask each group to take one of these purposes and brainstorm effective ways they could grade to satisfy this goal. The following ideas can be incorporated for each of the three purposes:

1. **Grade students' understanding:**
   - Develop a question to prompt kids' written responses (a paragraph or more) to the learning. This can be an exit ticket or a summation of one or more lessons. For example, if you have been teaching kids to take notes on a fact/question/response (F/Q/R) type of chart, you might ask them to use these to write about what they learned and what they thought about their learning in a paragraph or more.
   - In content classes, you can ask kids questions about what they learned. If they are using their strategies to read, listen, and view, you can grade them on what they have learned. If you have been teaching students to use comprehension strategies to learn information, they should understand the content much better than ever before because they are thinking about it. But rather than having them answer a multiple-choice question,

have them demonstrate their understanding by writing or drawing. For instance, after studying photosynthesis for several weeks, most kids can quite easily pick out the right multiple-choice answer to the question "What is photosynthesis?" But we are interested in deeper, more expansive learning and understanding, so asking students to demonstrate their understanding through a one-page written response to a question such as "How does photosynthesis impact your daily life?" shows a higher level of learning and understanding than merely answering a multiple-choice question. Understanding information and acquiring knowledge are the goals of comprehension instruction, not spitting out a memorized answer to a multiple-choice question.

2. **Hold students accountable:**
   - Come up with a grading scale for written responses, Post-its, thinksheets, and annotations—*not* on the initial lesson, but after kids have had a chance to practice. Some teachers develop evaluation criteria by asking these questions: Did students show evidence of understanding the strategy being used? Are there sufficient examples from which to judge? Did students meet most of the goals in the *Toolkit* lesson? The lesson's goals are not always met the first time students encounter the lesson, but as stated in the *Toolkit* Teacher's Guide, the lessons are really practices that are meant to be taught in many different texts and contexts over time. So we do expect kids to meet the goals of a lesson after they have had it several times and have been given time to practice. Another approach is to look at written responses over time. Assessment of work samples from the beginning and end of instruction on a strategy using the rubrics at the end of the book could be translated into grades to show progress over time.

3. **Satisfy the norms of school and society:**
   - Some schools require a certain number of grades per week. However, these don't have to come from strategy lessons. For example, if you taught inferring to help kids find and explain character traits, the grade could be given for a graphic organizer where they identify and explain character traits. The inferring was a prerequisite stepping stone to completing this task. Vocab-

ulary, writing, spelling, independent reading logs, reading response journals, and other aspects of the reading/language arts
block might also yield grades.

**Look closely at a *Toolkit*
lesson to move from
assessment to grades**
Ask teachers to apply the ideas they have for grading to the concrete example
of the lesson being discussed. We suggest Lesson 5, "Merge Thinking with
New Learning," in the *Activate & Connect* strategy book of the intermediate
*Toolkit*. Have them discuss ideas in groups and share.

# Ongoing Support

As you continue to work through each of the strategy books, return to this process of reviewing student work for assessment and planning for instruction as well as evaluating with the annotated rubric and suggestions from Part II of the workshop.

## Study Groups

- **Studying a variety of responses.** Watch the "Assessment" video on the CD-ROM with *The Comprehension Toolkit*. Discuss how Steph and Anne assess student work. Notice how they talk about student thinking and how they closely read the responses to gain a full understanding of what the student is doing as a reader. Also notice that they describe the context in which the responses occurred. We can't emphasize enough how important it is to view student work in relation to the instruction that was provided. After viewing and discussing the video, suggest that the participants pour over their "Assessment" sections of their *Toolkit* strategy books and flag different kinds of evidence of kids' learning. These will include Post-its, annotations, thinksheets, open-ended responses, posters, and other artifacts. Consider how important it is to encourage a wide variety of responses to gain a full picture of a child as a learner.

- **Assessing work samples.** Viewing and talking about student work samples can guide us in determining the next plans for instruction. Doing so in a collaborative group will accelerate the process. Ask each teacher to bring in three work samples from a single strategy lesson: one from a student who seems to have understood the task, one from a child who struggled, and one from a student who soared beyond the expectation.

  Provide copies of a "Reflect & Assess" section from any lesson, and discuss the analysis captions. Once you have discussed these, ask each teacher to present the work samples he or she has brought in. Follow up with a group discussion of what the samples show or do not show, and consider what the next step in teaching might be: Reteach? More practice? Challenge?

- **Evaluating work samples.** Remind participants that in that last session we assessed student work, discussing what we could infer from Post-its about what students did or did not understand. This time we'll look at the work samples to evaluate student learning. Working with their tablemates, have participants categorize the student responses into one of the three categories—strong evidence, some evidence, and little evidence—of strategy use. As they discuss their evaluations, circulate among the groups, listening and contributing to discussions. After discussing at their tables, have a few participants share out an example of where they placed the samples on the rubric and why.

■ **Planning the teaching-assessing loop.** *Toolkit* teaching requires that the teacher assess throughout the lesson; from Connect & Engage through Share the Learning, assessment is a 24/7 operation. The interaction that is built into *Toolkit* comprehension instruction allows teachers to stay on top of student thinking in order to guide the next steps of instruction. Teachers need to observe and listen to students as well as pay attention to students' responses at every stage of the lesson.

Ask teachers to select a *Toolkit* lesson, perhaps one that they will be teaching in the near future. Discuss the points at which teachers assess and look for evidence of student learning and thinking. The following chart may be useful to guide the conversation (see the *Staff Development Resources* CD-ROM).

| Assessing While Teaching | | |
|---|---|---|
| | **What I Want to Assess** | **What Kids Are Doing That Provides an Opportunity for Assessment** |
| Connect & Engage | | |
| Model | | |
| Guide | | |
| Collaborate | | |
| Practice Independently | | |
| Share the Learning | | |

Ask teachers to share what they look for during each part of the lesson. For example, a teacher may suggest that during the Connect & Engage part of the lesson, she tries to assess students' background knowledge for the topic, their understanding of vocabulary, and their level of engagement. She assesses this by listening to students turn and talk and by noticing the comments they share during the Connect & Engage portion.

Look at a lesson across these stages, and discuss other opportunities for assessment as the lesson unfolds.

### In-Class Coaching

- **When a teacher needs support to assess while teaching,** show how we assess students' understanding during instruction, carrying a clipboard for taking notes on individual students and collecting representative work samples. We use a kind of class form that focuses on the main objective of the lesson, and we jot our notes about student progress as we move around the room meeting with students and reading their responses. For example, an objective in intermediate *Toolkit* strategy book 5, *Determine Importance*, is that "[the student] codes the text to hold thinking, paraphrases, and records important information." As we confer with different students, we listen to them and look at their work in relation to this objective. Afterwards, debrief with the teacher. Review the collected work samples: What does each show? How might the results be recorded and kept? How might they be used to plan further instruction or student activities?

- **When a teacher needs support in interpreting student performance,** sit down together with a batch of work samples, and examine the evidence of the kids' thinking in relation to the current strategy being taught as well as their overall understanding of the text. (See also the first study group, assessing samples, above.) Depending on your samples and your goals—to look at individuals or the whole group, to focus on the strategy or on general understanding—you'll process the samples in different ways. The important thing is to think aloud as you begin, letting the teacher hear how you think through student work and then collaboratively discussing your questions, thoughts, and conclusions.

# Frequently Asked Questions

**How long should I give students to practice before I can evaluate their progress?**

This is definitely a tough question to answer, and you could ask five different people and receive five different answers. The easy answer is, "As much time as they need," but unfortunately we are rarely afforded that kind of time in education. So the answer comes more readily when additional questions are asked: (1) Does assessment tell you that students only need more time or need more time and support? (2) How much time are students afforded to practice the strategy within the school day? (3) In charting progress on a strategy, where are the students in relation to each other?

This last question is only included to help place performance in perspective. If most of the students in the classroom, with support and practice, are performing with strong evidence or some evidence, then it may be a time to evaluate. If most of the students in the classroom, with support and practice, are performing with little evidence, then you may not want to evaluate; instead, revisit the strategy, fine-tuning your instruction based on the student responses. The complexity of the strategy will most likely determine how long students should be given to practice. Teaching students to make connections will likely take less time than teaching them to determine importance. As an ending thought, two days on one strategy may not be enough, but two weeks may be too much. Trust your instincts and use student responses to inform your judgment.

For students who need quite a bit of additional teaching and practice, consider the *Comprehension Intervention* books, which provide small-group follow-up lessons for both the primary and intermediate *Toolkits*. These were written to support kids who need more time for practice, instruction, and individual attention

**How do I address the needs I see when I assess student work? What about the misconceptions students show?**

It's impossible to get back to students on every issue that arises as you review their work. If there are common misconceptions or confusions, they are worth reviewing with the whole class in a subsequent lesson.

## Frequently Asked Questions (continued)

It may be that you can pull a small group to address similar concerns that came up with only a handful of students. Some teachers write Post-its back to children when they return their work and are able to address some confusion this way in writing; then they follow up with those students during class by asking if they understood the Post-its. Others talk to kids when they first come to school in the morning or arrive in class while others are reading or doing a warm-up.

The good news is that when we read students' work and listen to what they say, their misconceptions surface. When students do conventional worksheets, their misconceptions may never see the light of day. By fostering a classroom culture where thinking is both audible and visible, we have a good shot at hearing and/or seeing our students' misconceptions. So stay tuned into the kids to be aware of their misconceptions and to be sure there is not a recurring pattern of confusion.

**I headed into Apollo Beach Elementary** one morning to meet with several teams of teachers who were focused on implementing the *Toolkits* with science and social studies topics. I was thrilled at the invitation as we had been working on *Toolkit* implementation in the literacy block for some time, and now I could support the teachers to take the next steps—to apply and use comprehension strategies across the curriculum. I had stressed that using the *Toolkits* in the content areas was one of the primary goals of *Toolkit* comprehension instruction, but saying it and doing it were very different things!

Today was the day to launch a science unit on life cycles with third grade. I opened our meeting by greeting teachers: "I can't tell you how excited I am to work with you on implementing *Toolkit* comprehension strategies in the content areas. The fact is we do not teach strategies for strategies' sake. We do not teach connecting to be the best connector in the room. We teach strategies so that our kids acquire and actively use knowledge. Teaching comprehension in science and social studies is ideal because when we think with and about the information, we truly understand and learn it. Content comprehension is our primary goal!"

After planning together for a few minutes, we headed off to the library to search for a book that would capture the kids' interest and hook them on life cycles. We found it in Brenda Guiberson's *Mud City: A Flamingo Story*, a narrative that follows the life cycle of the flamingo from egg to chick to maturity. It had all of the necessary requirements of a compelling read—unbelievable pictures, great text, and a built-in connection since we live in Florida and this book was about flamingos! We agreed that the science focus would be adaptation. To decide on a comprehension focus, we thought about what our kids would need most to understand the topic. When implementing *Toolkit* comprehension instruction with science and social studies, flexibility reigns supreme. We don't need to do the lessons in order; instead, we carefully choose the lesson that best meets the needs of the kids and the requirements of the text and topic.

We looked closely at the text and noticed words like *crèche, carotenoids, secrete*—vocabulary that might be unfamiliar to third graders—so we decided to teach "Inferring the Meaning of Unfamiliar Words," Lesson 10 in *The Comprehension Toolkit*. The teachers agreed that this lesson was crucial when introducing a new science unit because unfamiliar words and concepts often sink kids before they even get started. We pulled out the Lesson 10 Lesson Guide (pages 12–13) in the *Infer Meaning* strategy book and reviewed it because we planned to use it to guide our instruction with *Mud City*. The kids had all had this lesson in literacy but not in science, so we talked about how we might be able to shorten the introduction a little bit if they seemed to have a real understanding of the strategy. I reminded the teachers that these lessons were more practices than lessons and that they were designed to be taught multiple times, using the guide with different texts and topics. But I wanted them to understand that if kids were quite familiar with the strategy itself, they might not need all of the introductory explanation in the Lesson Guide.

The science teacher and I co-taught the demonstration lesson as the other third grade team members observed. We held the Lesson Guide in our laps and were thrilled to discover that the kids knew exactly what it was to infer. They remembered the inferring equation from previous *Toolkit* lessons! One student exclaimed, "This is what we do in reading all of the time. I just didn't know we were supposed to do the same thing in science!" So we moved into the text quickly and began to model how we crack unfamiliar vocabulary using the Model portion of the Lesson Guide.

As we modeled our thinking and read through the text, kids made connections throughout. When we read that flamingos secrete salt out of their eyelids, a young girl asked what it meant to secrete, so we modeled using context clues to infer the meaning of the word and then filled in our thinksheet accordingly. Once the meaning was clarified, she commented that the passage reminded her of the stinging sensation we experience when we get salty water in our eyes when swimming in the ocean. When we came upon the word *carotenoid* and inferred its meaning (a pigment that gives color to living things), a young boy connected the carotenoids making a flamingo pink to the way chlorophyll gives plants their greenish cast. The kids arrived at these powerful connections and new information because they were using the strategy of inferring to unlock unfamiliar vocabulary and concepts in science.

Over time, this third grade science teacher did eight science/literacy lessons with *Mud City*, some straight out of the *Toolkit* and others on writing in science. "I really understand now that hands-on science is not enough," she told me one day later that month. "Listening and reading about science enhance their understanding." And the truth is, it must be both hands-on and "minds-on" when it comes to science. *The Comprehension Toolkit* series gives our kids the tools they need to understand the information, and it helps them wrap their minds around science and social studies, thus expanding their thinking around the content.

# Introduction

## Content Literacy Across the Curriculum: What, Why, and When

While we tend to introduce *The Primary Toolkit* and *The Comprehension Toolkit* in the literacy block or during the reading period, our goal is to lay down a foundation of thinking and understanding across the curriculum throughout the year. The *Toolkit* strategies will support readers and thinkers to understand what they read and what they learn in science and social studies as well as in reading. The intention of the *Toolkits* is to teach for understanding and to engage kids in active literacy across the curriculum.

### What Is Content Literacy Across the Curriculum?

A major professional development goal is to get teachers to use the *Toolkits* routinely in the content areas. Too often our kids are just running their eyes across the page when reading content-area material. Just as they do in reading, kids need to stop, think, and react when they are reading in science and social studies. They need to connect, question, infer, and synthesize. Our kids need to spend much more time reading in the content areas so they can grasp the content, synthesize the information, and actively use the knowledge they gain. To support teachers to use the *Toolkits* in science and social studies, we encourage them to study and use the Lesson Guides at the end of each strategy lesson, to explore the content literacy portion of the *Extend & Investigate* book in *The Comprehension Toolkit*, to review "Using the *Toolkit* in Science and Social Studies" on pages 59–64 in *The Primary Toolkit*'s Teacher's Guide, and to watch and discuss the "Using the *Toolkit* in Science and Social Studies" PowerPoint presentation on the DVD-ROM in *The Primary Toolkit*.

### When Do Teachers Need Coaching in Content Literacy Across the Curriculum?

Teachers need coaching in content literacy if their students are simply not reading enough in the content areas and if there is evidence that they have not been taught to do so. Since much of what they will be reading both in and out of school will be authentic trade nonfiction and other genres that focus on content, asking them to read content-area material beyond the textbook will pay rich dividends. A few classroom observations during science and social studies time can inform a coach quickly as to the amount of content-area reading going on in the classroom, and truthfully it is not always a great deal. This lack of content-area reading affords an important coaching opportunity.

The *Toolkits* are very supportive when it comes to reading in science and social studies. The strategy book Lesson Guides—summaries of the teaching moves and teaching language at the end of every strategy lesson—are central to content-area reading. Supporting teachers to do *Toolkit* lessons, to use the Lesson Guides, to choose compelling content-area texts, to use the *Extend & Investigate* book, and to develop routines for regular content-area reading is a tall order. But we have found that once teachers see how much better their students understand science and social studies material when using comprehension strategies, they want to increase both the quantity and quality of the reading their kids do every day across the curriculum. Teachers also report that their kids become more engaged in content-area reading when using *Toolkit* comprehension strategies to help them get more from their reading. And last but not least, we find that students are more successful at reading and understanding complex content-area texts when they use comprehension strategies as they read. As always, this professional development will be most effective when teachers collaborate with one another and enlist the coach or literacy specialist to support them as they move forward.

# Workshop

## Session 1: Exploring Lesson Guides

This workshop includes three sessions. The first session focuses on exploring and analyzing the Lesson Guides at the end of each *Toolkit* lesson to provide comprehension instruction in the content areas. The second session explores a framework for integrating comprehension instruction with content units of study, a four-phase inquiry process as shared in the content literacy portions of the *Extend & Investigate* book in the Teacher's Guide in *The Primary Toolkit* and *The Comprehension Toolkit*. In the third session, teachers begin to plan a content unit matched to curricular standards with *Toolkit* comprehension strategies as the foundation.

### Purpose

To apply *Toolkit* lessons to science and social studies content

### Materials

*Ask teachers to bring:*

- One of these strategy books: *Activate & Connect* from *The Primary Comprehension Toolkit* or *Ask Questions* from *The Comprehension Toolkit*

- Trade book that relates to either their science or social studies content

*For the coach:*

- Same strategy books as the participants

- Document camera or interactive whiteboard to project the strategy book Lesson Guides as the teachers are looking at them

- Trade book or article with either a science or social studies focus (not a textbook section) that lends itself to teaching Lesson 7, "Merge Thinking with New Learning," in *The Primary Comprehension Toolkit* or Lesson 8, "Read to Discover Answers," in *The Comprehension Toolkit*

**Note:** A selection from the *Toolkit Texts* or a favorite nonfiction trade book would work well here. Brenda Guiberson's *Mud City* from the vignette at the beginning of this chapter is a good possibility. *Surprising Sharks* by Nicola Davies is another. Any book or article that you love that has a content focus will work for this workshop.

## *Workshop Steps*

**Share workshop goals**  Begin the session by asking teachers to turn and talk about how *Toolkit* instruction is going in their classrooms and to share whether they have tried using *Toolkit* instruction while teaching science and/or social studies. If so, how is it going?

Tell participants that they will be spending time in this workshop looking closely at the Lesson Guides at the end of each *Toolkit* lesson to analyze the language and moves and to figure out how to use the Lesson Guides to support them as they apply the strategy in a science and/or social studies trade book rather than in the *Toolkit* lesson text.

**Study a Lesson Guide**  Have teachers work in pairs to study a Lesson Guide and the lesson that precedes it. (For primary teachers, use Lesson 7, "Merge Thinking with New Learning," pages 46–61 in *Activate & Connect*. For intermediate teachers, use Lesson 8, "Read to Discover Answers," pages 12–25 in *Ask Questions*.) Call their attention to the relationship between the lesson and the Lesson Guide, prompting them to notice that the guide is the lesson with the content and text stripped away.

**Discuss the application of the Lesson Guides to content-area study**  Explain that the Lesson Guides are the Rosetta stone of the *Toolkits*, meaning that they connect the *Toolkit* language to any content-rich text and do it in a way that makes the *Toolkits* generative. The Lesson Guides are cheat sheets in a way. They are scaffolds for doing the lesson with your own text and topics, so they are the perfect support for providing a *Toolkit* lesson in the content area.

Project the Lesson Guide from one of the strategy lessons on the document camera or interactive whiteboard. Have the teachers look at the Connect & Engage section of the Lesson Guide as you walk them through the language and moves. Ask them to consider how this might play out in one of their science or social studies texts.

**Observe the use of a Lesson Guide with a content-area text**  Model using the Lesson Guide with the text you brought in. Read the text aloud, and work through the Model section of the lesson, using the language of the guide with the content of the text that you brought with you.

**Introduce and teach a strategy with a Lesson Guide**  Ask participants to study the Lesson Guide at the end of their lesson in relation to the text they brought in. How would they *connect and engage* their kids with this text? How would they *model* the strategy using the first page(s) or another excerpt? Encourage them to incorporate the teaching moves and the teaching language into their plan.

Then have teachers pair up and use the Lesson Guide to practice the lesson on each other with their content-area text.

**Define next steps**  Wrap up by inviting teachers to share what they learned and anything they wonder about. What was easy about using the Lesson Guide? What was challenging?

Then encourage them to try a lesson in their own classrooms using a Lesson Guide and a nonfiction text they have chosen. Ask them to teach a science or social studies topic and come to the next workshop session ready to talk about their experience. Next, encourage teachers to demonstrate for each other in their own classrooms, taking turns modeling and observing. Ask them to keep track of what they notice and wonder as they watch each other. They can use a two-column form with one column titled "Observations" and the second column titled "Questions."

# Session 2: Understanding Inquiry Framework

## Purpose
To use a four-phase inquiry framework and comprehension strategies to understand and learn about science and social studies units and topics

## Materials
*For each participant:*
- Copy of "Hallmarks for Creating an Environment for Thoughtful Content Literacy Instruction" (*The Primary Comprehension Toolkit*, Teacher's Guide, page 61)

*Ask teachers to bring:*
- For intermediate teachers, their *Extend & Investigate* book
- For primary teachers, their Teacher's Guide

*For the coach:*
- All the participants' materials
- *The Primary Comprehension Toolkit* DVD-ROM
- Computer or DVD player on which to play and project the DVD-ROM
- Document camera

## Workshop Steps

**Discuss content-area teaching experiences**

Begin by having the participants turn and talk about how things went as they taught some *Toolkit* lessons with science and social studies texts. Ask them to talk first about what went well and then to talk about the challenges. (It is in our DNA to go to the challenges first, so as coaches, we need to suggest that they talk first about the opportunities and then the challenges.) Have them share out their experiences in trying to implement *Toolkit* comprehension instruction in science and/or social studies. Also ask anyone who worked with a partner in their classroom to share anything they gleaned from that experience.

**Share workshop goals**

Explain that participants will spend time today learning about a framework for content literacy so they can begin to use the *Toolkits* when planning and implementing content-area units.

**Read "Hallmarks for Creating an Environment for Thoughtful Content Literacy Instruction"**

Distribute copies of the hallmarks (*The Primary Comprehension Toolkit* Teacher's Guide, page 61), and display one on a document camera for the whole group to see. Assign each of five groups or pairs one of the five big ideas on the page:

1. "The learning opportunities we create . . . ,"
2. "When we demonstrate our thinking . . . ,"
3. "We support attitudes and interactions . . . ,"
4. "Student artifacts and work products . . . ,"
5. "Materials, texts, and literature . . . ,"

Let them read through and discuss each of the bullet points beneath their assigned idea for a couple of minutes. Then have each pair or group share their thoughts with the whole group so they can all hear the thinking behind each of the big ideas.

**View a slideshow of a content-area unit**

Show the "Reading, Writing, and Research in Science and Social Studies" PowerPoint on *The Primary Comprehension Toolkit* DVD-ROM to all participants, ending with slide 60. Explain that even though the examples are for K–2, intermediate content comprehension looks similar. Use these two steps:

1. On slide 21, have teachers turn and talk about how to create environments that foster thinking and understanding. Suggest that

intermediate teachers think about how this would look in intermediate classrooms.

2. On slide 60, have them turn and talk with a partner about how these practices could work with their own content-area units.

**Study overviews of the inquiry framework**

Share the chart that lays out ways that *Toolkit* lessons support content-area inquiry. Have primary teachers turn to pages 62–63 in their *Toolkit* Teacher's Guides. Ask intermediate teachers to turn to pages 10–11 in *Extend & Investigate*. Display one or the other on the document camera, and take participants through the framework by sharing each of the four phases. (They are labeled differently in the two resources, but point out that they are essentially the same.) Note that the chart is set up to show what the teacher is doing and what the kids are doing in each phase. Point out the *Toolkit* lesson links. These are among the most supportive pieces in the content literacy portion because they help teachers choose which lessons to do with which phase of the content-area study process.

Once you have highlighted an example from each phase, have teachers work through these two-page spreads with a partner to get a grasp of the nitty-gritty of content comprehension.

**Debrief the inquiry framework**

Wrap up by inviting comments on the framework and having teachers think about how they might use the inquiry framework and *Toolkit* comprehension strategies to implement a content unit. Ask them to discuss which science or social studies units they have coming up that might best lend themselves to this approach.

# Session 3: Planning a Content-Area Unit

In preparation for planning a content-area unit in this workshop, teachers will need to have selected a science or social studies unit they want to develop. Tell them ahead of time to select an upcoming unit to approach using the inquiry framework. They will need to gather books and articles related to their unit in addition to having on hand the content standards in use in their schools. You might also want to prepare a "volunteer" ahead of time to help you model the planning process for the group.

## Purpose

To plan content literacy instruction in a science or social studies unit using the inquiry framework

## Materials

*For each participant:*

- Copy of the content literacy section from *The Comprehension Toolkit, Extend & Investigate*, pages 8–22

*Ask teachers to bring:*

- *Toolkit* Teacher's Guide (either primary or intermediate)

- School or district standards for a content unit they have chosen to plan

- Some books or articles related to that content unit

*For the coach:*

- All participants' materials

- Document camera

## *Workshop Steps*

**Share workshop goals**  Explain that today's objective is to leave with a partially developed plan for using the *Toolkit* inquiry framework to teach one of their own science or social studies units.

**Review the inquiry framework**  Distribute the copies of the content literacy section of *The Comprehension Toolkit's Extend & Investigate* (pages 8–22). Explain that we will be using this topic-study model to guide our planning. Have teachers review the research phases with a partner and talk about how they see the inquiry framework playing out in their science and social studies instruction.

**Look at sample topic studies**

Direct teachers' attention to the "Topic Study in Action" sections on pages 12–15 and 16–19 in their content literacy handout. Explain that there is one example of a social studies unit on Western expansion for upper intermediate and another example of a science unit on extreme weather for lower intermediate grades. Note that these units of study follow the inquiry framework and integrate comprehension instruction with content during the research process. Explain that it does not matter whether they actually teach these content units; they are merely a model for unit study.

Have participants review these samples with a partner. The primary teachers should concentrate on the extreme weather unit because it is closer to their grade levels, and the upper intermediate teachers should focus their attention on the Western expansion unit.

**Observe the planning process**

While participants are looking at the sample topic studies in action, invite a volunteer to bring texts for his or her unit and the related content standards to the front of the room and work with you to plan a content unit of study with the blank Topic Study Guide (pages 20–22 of the content literacy handout).

Once participants have finished reviewing the sample "Topic Study in Action," place a copy of the Topic Study Guide (page 20 of the handout) on the document camera, and talk with the teacher volunteer about the large concepts and essential questions related to the standards for the unit he or she has brought in. List them in the allotted space.

Explain that this Topic Study Guide is only designed for one or two lessons in each phase of the framework but that when they fully develop their unit's content literacy plan, they will likely teach a number of lessons for building background, gathering information, and so on.

With one of the texts that the volunteer teacher brought in, begin to craft a lesson plan on the Topic Study Guide under the "Build Background Knowledge Through Exploration" section of the framework. Refer to pages 12 and 16 in the handout as a scaffold for planning instruction. It is often helpful to begin a content unit of study with Lesson 1 in either *Toolkit*, although Lesson 7 in *The Primary Comprehension Toolkit* and Lesson 5 in *The Comprehension Toolkit* are also powerful first lessons as we launch a content unit of study.

**Plan a content unit**

Tell teachers that now it is their turn. Suggest that they use the summary chart of *Toolkit* lessons in their *Toolkit* Teacher's Guides (pages 38–39 in *The Primary Comprehension Toolkit* Teacher's Guide; pages 22–23 in *The Compre-*

*hension Toolkit* Teacher's Guide) so they have all of the lessons at their finger-tips as they plan content literacy instruction. Mention that these two-page spreads are among the most important pages in the *Toolkits* because they provide the big picture of the whole array of *Toolkit* lessons.

Have teachers work through the blank Topic Study Guide choosing a lesson, a text, and a plan for each of the next three phases in the inquiry framework. Move around the room and confer with individuals or pairs as they create their content literacy plans.

**Share plans**    Wrap up by having volunteers share one quadrant of the framework, the text they will use, and the lesson they intend to do.

# Ongoing Support

## *Study Groups*

- **Book studies.** Suggest a few possible book studies. *Comprehension Going Forward*, an edited volume of chapters from a range of authors who specialize in comprehension theory and practice, includes several chapters that relate directly to content literacy. Chapter 8, "History Lessons," by Anne Goudvis and Brad Buhrow shows how teachers have merged comprehension instruction with history to support students to better understand and engage in history topics. Chapter 9, "Comprehension in Science," by Gina Cervetti details how to combine science content with comprehension instruction to build scientific thinkers. For a longer read, *Comprehension and Collaboration: Inquiry Circles in Action* is a great study-group book for teachers who are interested in inquiry-based learning in science and social studies. It dovetails nicely with *Toolkit* instruction and goes into more explicit detail about the collaboration strategies that we see in the *Toolkits*.

- **Choice of text and lessons for content units of study.** Invite teachers to this study group, and ask them to bring some texts (no textbooks) that they would like to use as they create instruction for a content unit of study. Begin the study group by sharing two quite difficult, complex articles for the teachers themselves, one with a science focus and one with a history focus. Do a short book talk on each one of the articles, and encourage them to choose one to read silently, annotate it as they read, and then discuss with a partner who read the same article.

  Once they have finished their discussion, ask them to share what they noticed themselves doing as readers to understand the article. The *Toolkit* strategies will emerge as they share what was happening when they read. Jot them down and create a list on the document camera as they share out. The participants will also likely report some emotional reactions to the content. Add those to the list as well. Explain that when we peel back the layers of our own content reading process, we glean a better understanding of what reading is all about. Once they have shared out their reading process, ask them to think about and report what happened in their discussion. Also jot down those comments, which are likely to include things such as "I felt validated," "I got a question answered," and "We had different ideas about what was important here."

Have teachers read through some of the texts they brought in for their units of study, and encourage them to think about their own thinking as they read them, just as they did when reading the adult texts earlier in this study group. This will lead to a better understanding of what they should be teaching when they read these texts with kids. Keep the two-page summary charts from the *Toolkit* Teacher's Guides (*The Primary Comprehension Toolkit*, pages 38–39; *The Comprehension Toolkit*, pages 22–23) close at hand, and encourage teachers to think about which texts to use with different lessons. Some lessons are better with science-oriented content; others are better with historical texts. For instance, Lesson 25, "Reread and Rethink," in *The Comprehension Toolkit* is particularly useful when reading history texts, and Lesson 5, "Merge Your Thinking with New Learning," is very useful for science reading.

As the participants are looking at the texts and searching for a good lesson match, you can move about the room checking in with individuals and pairs, adding support and addressing their concerns. Facilitate a conversation about which lessons are the most important for science reading and which are central to history reading, and co-construct a list of about six lessons that are the most powerful for each content area (there may be some overlap here). As they apply *Toolkit* strategies to the content areas, they may not need to do each and every *Toolkit* lesson; instead, they can do the lessons that appear to be most suited to their content-area reading.

Also spend time in this study group guiding participants to search for additional high-quality texts that match the content-area focus. Have them look at the trade book bibliographies in *The Comprehension Toolkit*'s *Extend & Investigate* book (pages 127–139) and the bibliographies in *The Primary Comprehension Toolkit*'s *Keep Reading! Source Book* (pages 139–155). Suggest that teachers go online and check out some of the websites listed in these bibliographies, as well as others they know about. Co-create a list of websites that are not included in the *Toolkits* as an additional resource.

■ **Content literacy monitoring.** Few schools have kids reading enough in language arts, let alone in the content areas. Read

Chapter 12, "Reading for Understanding in Social Studies and Science," in *Strategies That Work* to build background on content-area reading. Upon completion of the chapter, have participants discuss the information. Ask them to speculate about how much time their kids are spending each week reading science and social studies material that they can and want to read; have them write down the number of minutes. Explain that in order to begin to sort out how much reading is actually going on in science and social studies, the first step is to audit the amount of time kids actually spend reading accessible science and social studies texts. Give each teacher two copies of the Content Literacy Monitoring Sheet, one for science and one for social studies (see the *Staff Development Resources* CD-ROM), and ask them to track the amount of time kids spend reading, writing, and talking in the content areas for one week. Show them how to fill it in so they have a good idea of how it works when they begin to keep track of the time kids actually spend reading, writing, and talking in the content areas that week. Plan to review this form when you meet with them for an in-class coaching session.

■ **Genre of textbook reading.** This is a study group for intermediate and middle school teachers. Ask everyone to read "The Genre of Textbook Reading" section of *Extend & Investigate*, pages 23–30, before they come to the first study-group meeting. Spend the first meeting discussing what they have learned. Focus on pages 26–28, which are related to the critical consumer guide. Have them review the criteria and brainstorm additional criteria for this guide.

For the next meeting, ask participants to read through the model lessons on pages 31–72 in *Extend & Investigate* ahead of time. When they come in for the next meeting, have them focus and expand on "Using the Textbook," pages 29–30. Facilitate a discussion of the information here. Then jigsaw the lessons, asking them to get into pairs and review two lessons each. Assign groups so that all of the lessons are covered, and then have them read through, study, and talk about the two lessons they were assigned.

Finally, have teachers bring in their textbooks and look at each lesson to discover how they would apply that sample lesson to their own textbooks. They will find that some of the lessons work better than others, depending on the nature of their particular textbook. Make sure the participants understand that as with all types of reading, textbook reading will benefit kids if they are thinking about it and making strategic decisions as they go.

- **Genre of test reading.** This is a study group for intermediate and middle school teachers, and it focuses on helping kids think their way through standardized tests. With any form of reading, readers do better if they are thinking about what they are reading. It is the same with test reading. Share with the participants that tests are truly their own genre—and an increasingly important genre at that. Using "The Genre of Test Reading" section of the *Extend & Investigate* book, pages 73–84, focus first on the test reading tips (pages 75–77). Have the participants read through the tips with a partner. Make it clear that these are generic tips for multiple-choice standardized reading tests and that although these tips will help kids in all tests, their state tests may have additional characteristics that pertain only to those tests, so they will also need to make sure their kids understand the particulars of their state tests.

    Guide teachers as they review the four different types of test questions on pages 78–79. Have them divide into four groups and jigsaw the four different types of questions—vocabulary, literal, summarizing and synthesizing, and inferential. Once they have looked carefully at one group of questions, encourage each group to share out what they noticed about that specific type of test question.

    Finally, have participants turn to pages 82–83 and take the test, paying attention to how they think through the test and figure out what to focus on as they answer the questions. Suggest that they annotate their thinking in the margins. Once they have all finished thinking through the test, have them turn to pages 80–81 and compare their thinking to Steph and Anne's thinking process.

## In-Class Coaching

- **When teachers begin to increase the amount of reading kids do in science and social studies,** a terrific in-class coaching opportunity emerges. First off, kids need to be reading in content texts they can read. So rolling up our sleeves and helping teachers find a wide range of interesting content-area texts on a variety of levels to cover all of the readers in their classes are paramount. During the pre-lesson conference, talk about how to arrange these texts in the most accessible way so that kids can easily avail themselves of them, perhaps put in baskets at tables or placed around the room where kids can quickly and efficiently get their hands on them.

Go over the Content Literacy Monitoring Sheet that was introduced in the study group. Ask teachers to compare what they found in relation to what they speculated in terms of time spent reading in the content area. Ask what, if anything, surprised them about the audit. Ask how they will respond to this newfound information.

Then, in front of the teachers, model a lesson on choosing a content-area text that is just right for the students. Bring three content-area texts to the lesson: a book that is challenging, an article that is easy, and a text that is just right. To model choosing a just-right text for the kids, hold up the challenging text and explain that in a text that is too hard, you can't read a lot of the words and can't understand most of the ideas. Show an easy text and explain that in an easy text, you can read all of the words and understand all of the ideas. Then share a text that is just right. Explain that a just-right text is one where you can read most of the words and understand most of the ideas. Once you have modeled how to choose a just-right text, have kids choose a book and send them off to read independently with a text they chose based on this new approach. Move around the room and confer with kids to check on their book selection. Once you have completed the demonstration lesson, debrief with the teachers, asking them to look carefully at the kids' choices to determine whether they think the kids chose a just-right book.

# Frequently Asked Questions

**Do I have to provide comprehension instruction as well as teach content? Won't it take so long that I won't cover what I need to?**

Content-area teachers often chose to become content specialists because they loved their content—after all, if they wanted to be reading teachers, they would have specialized in reading. In addition, few content-area teachers were taught the ins and outs of teaching reading. But alas, if kids are not taught to read content material, there is little reason to read it at all. Content-area reading is among the most complex of all texts, and for that reason, students need strategies to understand what they read. The more challenging the text, the more strategic the reader must be. But don't despair; believe it or not, there is no one better to teach science reading than the science teacher and no one better to teach history reading than the history teacher. Science teachers read a lot of science material, and history teachers read a lot of history material, so begin by peeling away the layers of your own reading process and share with the kids what you do as a reader of science or history. Take a look at pages 38–39 in the primary *Toolkit* Teacher's Guide and pages 22–23 in the intermediate *Toolkit* Teacher's Guide at the spreads that show all of the lessons in the *Toolkits*. Choose several that you think would be most important for your content area, and begin with those. Teachers tell us that once they see how much better their students understand what they read, they are ready to teach even more comprehension lessons. Ultimately, it is about going slow to go fast. Yes, it takes a little extra time to teach content comprehension at first, but most kids understand so much more of their content-area reading that it saves time in the long run.

**I work with a science specialist. How can I coordinate content literacy teaching with this teacher?**

*The Comprehension Toolkit* lends itself to collaboration. We want all of our kids to participate in the *Toolkit* launch lessons. We work very hard to make sure that no child is pulled out of the whole-group *Toolkit* lesson for any reason, such as visits with specialists, special education programs, or English language learning classes, so articulation and communication between the specialist and the classroom teacher are

## Frequently Asked Questions (continued)

imperative. When the kids go to science lab, we make sure that the science specialist knows what strategy we are currently working on and the most recent lesson so that the specialist can echo that lesson in the science lab. If we have just taught "Read and View with a Question in Mind" in the classroom, the science specialist can focus on that strategy when the kids are reading and viewing in the science lab. This reinforcement and application of the strategy in science are very powerful for students. So collaboration is key, and yes, it takes a village!

# Afterword: Growing a *Toolkit* Project

## Joanne Durham

**This afterword describes** the carefully designed efforts of the members of another large, diverse school district, the Prince George's County Public Schools in Maryland, as they worked to foster teacher knowledge and expertise in teaching reading comprehension. Joanne Durham, Coordinator of Special Instructional Programs, and her colleagues created ways to implement *The Comprehension Toolkits* with their mandated basal programs. They wanted to ensure that their students would engage in thoughtful comprehension learning, and they believed that challenging and robust comprehension instruction would enhance the program curriculum and standards already in place. As a literacy coordinator who lives the everyday reality of doing what's best for kids under challenging circumstances and nonstop demands, Joanne weaves in many of the practices shared in this book to demonstrate how to develop a community of "teachers as learners" in a district. What better way to ensure that teachers continue to take the lead in transforming classroom practices?

Good ideas grow in fertile soil. In the school district in which I work, we experience all the challenges of large and diverse urban school systems. We also have many dedicated teachers who want to change the trajectory for our bright and capable kids. It's been my privilege over the past five years to lead a Title I project working with teachers centered on *The Comprehension Toolkit*. Many teachers, principals, literacy specialists, and district coaches have participated in these efforts, and we have been able to watch the good ideas from the *Toolkits* grow deep roots among our staff and students.

## Beginning with Sound Theories

It took us awhile to figure out that the *Toolkit* approach was the one to take. As a large school system with high student mobility and teacher turnover, we use a basal reading program to provide continuity. But we also recognize the necessity of keeping up with the latest thinking in literacy instruction and of integrating what we learn into our program. So when we did a year-long book study of *Mosaic of Thought* by Ellin Keene and Susan Zimmermann with all the school-based elementary reading specialists in our county in the early 2000s, the enthusiasm was palpable. We had been talking about reading comprehension strategies for a while, but this was different. *Mosaic* unearthed what is really happening when we adults read to understand, and it made us appreciate the importance of letting our students into the "reading club." Despite our best efforts up to that time, we felt that our students were still mainly outsiders, sometimes dutifully answering the comprehension questions and creating graphic organizers but not sharing in the depth of thought and interaction that characterized our own book discussions.

Simultaneously, we discovered *Strategies That Work (STW)*, and in this book, Stephanie Harvey and Anne Goudvis more directly showed us how

## We root staff development in shared professional study.

to teach comprehension strategies to children. We began school-based study groups on *STW*, organized by our regional resource teachers (RRTs) and school-based reading specialists. Anne Goudvis came and led a workshop for teachers who had begun working with *STW*—bringing her well-traveled posters plastered with Post-its and the student drawings expressing children's thinking on so many topics—and sparked even greater enthusiasm among us.

Then one day some of the RRTs came to me and said, "Joanne, you have to check out the latest from Harvey and Goudvis, *The Comprehension Toolkit*. It's *STW* on steroids! It gives actual teacher moves and teacher language for strategy lessons with nonfiction texts."

Wanting to focus and develop this work, we created a pilot project to integrate the *Toolkits* into our reading programs. We were able to arrange for Anne to return several times across the school year to work with a group of coaches, reading specialists, and 11 teachers in five schools. The seeds of our project were planted.

Now we are in our fifth year, and over 300 teachers in 30 Title I schools use *The Primary Comprehension Toolkit* for grades K–2 or *The Comprehension Toolkit* for grades 3–6. By the third year, we had formed a leadership group of teachers, coaches, and reading specialists who meet regularly to sum up our progress, lay future plans, and provide professional development sessions and demonstration lessons. Our middle school colleagues recognized the difference in students coming to them and began to integrate *Toolkit* lessons into their curriculum frameworks. The *Toolkits* underlie how we think about providing both the challenge and support needed to allow our students to reach their full capabilities as literate learners.

## Learning from the *Toolkits*

As we studied the *Toolkits*, we recognized several ways we wanted to teach comprehension strategies differently from how they were laid out and organized in our basal program. The major differences are summarized in Table 1 and discussed below.

| Before *Comprehension Toolkit*, We . . . | With *Comprehension Toolkit*, We . . . |
|---|---|
| Spiraled through a different comprehension strategy each week | Begin with inner conversation, spend several weeks focusing on each strategy in a logical order, and return to integrating strategies fourth quarter |
| | Expect and support students to use all previously learned strategies along with the focus one |
| Reviewed the same thing about a strategy each time we taught it | Scaffold deeper understanding of the strategy with each lesson |
| Used terminology of the basal reader to describe strategies | Use terminology of *The Comprehension Toolkit* to describe strategies |
| Provided an occasional, brief think-aloud for a strategy, per basal reader suggestions | Use gradual release of responsibility to engage, model/think aloud, guide, collaboratively/independently practice, share, and assess |
| | Use language and teaching moves from the *Toolkits* |
| Spent very little time on strategy instruction and mostly focused on tested skills | Focus first on strategies to access new texts and then revisit for tested skills |
| Spent the majority of time on fiction | Spend equal time on fiction and nonfiction |
| Did not integrate strategies into content areas | Integrate strategies into content areas |

Table 1: Contrasting ways of teaching comprehension

The development of lessons in each *Toolkit* strategy book opened our eyes to the nuances of each strategy and the logical scaffolding of students' facility with using them. For example, instead of teaching inferring the same way each time, we developed the strategy as the *Toolkits* do: beginning with inferring at the word level with vocabulary in context and continuing to take inferring to deeper levels through inferring ideas, figurative language, answers to questions, and eventually themes. This scaffolding was particularly helpful with determining importance. We had struggled so often with teaching students to "find the main idea," without realizing how helpful it would be to teach them first to slow down and think about new information through the Fact/Question/Response (F/Q/R) process and then move on to distinguishing important information from interesting ideas and distinguishing the reader's thinking from the author's. All of these steps led students to a greater understanding of what's important in their reading.

Another important change with using the *Toolkits* was viewing monitoring as an umbrella over all the strategies, not as an isolated concept. By beginning the year with the "inner conversation," we helped students see that strategies are various ways people think when they are fully engaged with texts and that good readers use them flexibly. We began to dispel the "if it's Tuesday, we must be questioning" phenomenon, whereby students gave us the strategy we were looking for, not because it was useful to them but because it was the focus of the week.

> **We embrace new ways of thinking about thinking— and about teaching.**

Finally, our instruction on strategies changed dramatically once we began using the *Toolkits*. We moved from one or two examples given by the teacher in a lesson to entire lessons devoted to the strategy, using the gradual release of responsibility. Rather than framing students' thinking with the questions from the basal reader teacher's edition, the gradual release approach allowed students' own thinking to become central. The teaching moves and teaching language in the *Toolkits* made a huge difference in the support we offered students to actually use strategies to interact with what they were reading.

## Integrating the *Toolkits* into Our Intermediate Grade Reading Program

By the middle of the first year, we were seeing big changes with the students. Their enthusiasm for reading was way up, and struggling readers, special education students, and ELL learners were demonstrating their thinking in conversation and on Post-its in ways that they had never done before. The work also provided the opportunity for many of our teachers to blossom. They were excited to find an approach that matched their intuitive sense of how their classrooms should function—the genuine student participation, the collaborative community, the emphasis on strengths of all children, the focus on thinking rather than single right answers. But in addition to genuine student and teacher engagement, we needed to meet the practical necessities of established standards and the assessments based on them.

Since the beginning of No Child Left Behind and the creation of our state's standards, our district has created curriculum frameworks that merge our basal materials with the reading skills that will appear on our state tests. During the first year we used *The Comprehension Toolkit*, we simply made suggestions for how teachers in our pilot project could substitute *Toolkit* lessons that generally fit within our curriculum framework for those in their basal reader. However, as we met together throughout the year, we realized that with each teacher figuring out how to integrate the *Toolkits* into the basal program, we duplicated a lot of effort and took a great deal of time. So we began to lay plans to create a curriculum framework specifically for the *Toolkit* schools.

### Creating a Curriculum Framework

We gathered teachers and coaches who were using the resources and hashed out the general outline of our framework. We knew we had to address all the major reading objectives from our state standards, since these form the basis for our high-stakes annual tests. While the thematic approach of our basal has certain advantages, we thought we could better teach our students to apply comprehension strategies if we organized around genres so that we could stick with a strategy for a few weeks at a time in the same type of text. Our plan was to use the basal reader for the reading selections, vocabulary, background support, and comprehension skills where possible while strengthening the strategy work with *The Comprehension Toolkit*. We also recognized that we would need to supplement the basal with additional nonfiction selections, since there weren't enough short nonfiction pieces that would fit well with each strategy. Then we set up a timetable for teaching all the strategies before our March test. After testing, we planned to integrate strategies to be sure that students understood that while we spent time focusing on one strategy or another, readers use them at point of need, not because they are assigned by the teacher.

Our curriculum framework begins with two weeks of establishing the rituals and routines of an effective literacy classroom, and we found that the *Monitor Comprehension* strategy book lessons fit seamlessly into those back-to-school sessions. Teaching students to follow their inner conversation, notice when they lose their way, and use read/write/talk set up the expectations for what strategies are and established practices to be used throughout the year. We added specific lessons to teach kids to turn and talk and to use strategies in their daily independent reading. From there, we proceeded to determine lessons to use from the rest of the strategy books.

**With comprehension strategies at the center, we build a curriculum framework and a timetable to prepare for standards-based assessment.**

With a March assessment deadline, we could not include every lesson from every book, so we chose those we thought most necessary and sometimes combined lessons. We found the order of the strategy books, with each new lesson and book building on and integrating the previous ones, helpful in scaffolding the development of strategy use, so we stuck with it. The *Toolkit* lessons focus on nonfiction, but we knew that most of the strategies pertained to fiction as well, so we decided that the strategy books would form the skeleton for our units, and we would adapt *Toolkit* lessons to fiction where they were applicable.

| Comprehension Strategy/Genre | Approximate Number of Weeks |
|---|:---:|
| Monitor Comprehension | 2 |
| Nonfiction—Activate/Connect, Question | 5 |
| Fiction—Infer and Visualize | 7 |
| Nonfiction—Determine Importance | 6 |
| Nonfiction—Summarize and Synthesize | 2 |
| Fiction—Summarize and Synthesize | 2 |
| State Testing Window— Preparation and Administration | 3 |
| Fiction¬ and Nonfiction— Integrating Strategies | 10 |

Table 2: Organization and timing of units

As we reviewed the *Toolkit* lessons we had included in our framework, we found that about two-thirds of the state standards had been met just through the strategy lessons. After all, making inferences and determining importance are at the heart of the vast majority of comprehension skills. A tested skill of identifying character traits, for example, is mostly a matter of inferring. Seldom does an author tell us that "John is timid." Instead, the writer describes John sinking down into his seat and hiding his face; the reader infers that he is shy. Once we paired teaching character traits with inferring, it made much more sense. Too often our instruction had focused just on what character traits are and had ignored the thinking process of inferring that goes into actually discovering them in texts. So we developed a teaching cycle over a week or more in which we began by teaching comprehension strategies to support overall understanding of a new text (e.g., inferring), moved to revisiting the text to look at specific components of our standards (e.g., identifying and explaining character traits), and then transferred the learning to small-group sessions while using texts differentiated to reading levels or to readers' interests and choices.

## Tailoring the *Toolkits* to Our Own Needs

Next, we correlated the *Toolkit* lessons we had chosen with appropriate texts. Our first choices were the texts that were used in the *Toolkit* lessons so that teachers would be able to first try the lesson as it had been taught by Stephanie or Anne. However, we didn't want to repeat the same texts over grade levels, so we assigned each of the *Toolkit* texts to one grade and searched for alternate texts for the other grades. For fiction, we mainly used the selections from the basal as well as some additional trade books we knew and loved. For nonfiction, we found a few selections in our basal anthology but also chose texts from the *Source Book of Short Text, Toolkit Texts*, and additional sources such as *Time for Kids* collections, web magazine databases, and trade books. We wanted to be sure we had the most engaging texts that required clear use of the targeted strategy to aid in developing meaning. Our basal also matched anthology selections with three leveled readers, so these were helpful for differentiated texts for additional small-group practice.

Once we had identified texts, we gathered teachers, coaches, and reading specialists together and began to write sample lessons. We created a lesson-planning template outlining the stages of gradual release. We read the *Toolkit* lesson—not only the abbreviated Lesson Guide but the complete lesson as taught—very carefully. We wanted to fully understand what the purpose of the lesson was, how it built on previous lessons, and how it scaffolded future ones.

We also paid particular attention to the conversational language Stephanie and Anne used in specific *Toolkit* lessons. We discussed how the lesson language emphasizes the many choices students make as they record their thinking—ideas of their own that may be similar to or different from others' and questions or responses shared *if they have one* (*not* because they have to fill out every box in a graphic organizer). We discussed how the language helps put the students in charge of their work. The *Toolkits* prompt them to do it out of interest, curiosity, and a sense of reading purpose, and we wanted to capture those attributes in our sample lessons with different texts.

**We embrace the *Toolkit* model to select additional texts, create new lessons, and structure time for literacy.**

We designed our lessons to be samples, not scripts to be followed verbatim, but we wrote them out as completely as possible to provide the same kind of modeling that the *Toolkit* lessons gave us. The overall feedback from teachers was positive, as long as their administrators were clear that these sample lessons are guides and not prescriptions. The teachers generally followed the lessons rather closely as they were learning *Toolkit* moves and language; once they internalized these, they began to deviate much more and make the lessons their own. We encouraged them to do so—to capture the authenticity of their own thinking and to share it with their students.

It was important to balance strategy instruction with other needs in the reading/language arts block, including writing, differentiated guided reading groups, vocabulary, and word work. We created some samples of time use to facilitate these decisions. Some teachers found that long stretches of strategy work with modeling, guiding, and collaborating over a couple of days worked best for them, whereas others liked shorter stretches across more days. Many factors—departmentalization, ELLs, and special education schedules among them—influenced their decisions.

Developing a curriculum framework for integrating the *Toolkits* with our basal reader took a lot of work, but it clarified some important issues. The framework gave schools confidence that they were meeting the required state standards when they used the *Toolkits*. It helped them put the *Toolkits* into perspective in relation to the entire reading/language arts program. The *Toolkits* aren't the only thing we do in our literacy block. Nonetheless, schools have come to refer to themselves as "*Toolkit* schools" because the *Toolkit* work underlies everything else they do. The community they build, the charts they hang on the walls, and the way teachers talk to kids reflect the principles of active literacy whether it is *Toolkit* time or not.

## Summary: Steps for Integrating the *Toolkits* into an Intermediate Grade Reading Program

- Define the differences between the current approach to teaching comprehension and the *Toolkit* approach, and clarify the reasons for making the change.

- Develop an organizational structure based on the *Toolkit* strategy books, and identify which *Toolkit* lessons are most important to include. (This might change as you teach!)

- Identify the Common Core State Standards or specific state standards met by the *Toolkit* lessons, and determine where additional teaching for specific expectations is needed.

- Correlate the *Toolkit* lessons with the additional standards so that the strategies provide the thinking students need to work with literary or nonfiction constructs they are expected to know.

- Identify the text resources from the basal—or other materials currently in use—that support what you plan to teach, and correlate them with the lessons.

- Identify additional needed resources (if any) to support the teaching plan, and correlate them with the lessons. Possibly assign the texts used in the *Toolkit* lessons to specific grades so that teachers at every grade have the opportunity to try out the lessons with the direct support of the *Toolkits*.

- Create some sample lessons with the texts you have selected using the *Toolkit* lessons as a guide. Stay true to the teaching language and teaching moves of the *Toolkits*.

- Do a reality check on your expectations. Will all the lessons fit into the time allotted for teaching literacy? Provide suggestions for comprehension lesson timing if your teachers need guidance in how to fit it all in.

## Integrating the *Toolkits* into Our Primary Grade Reading Program

Our approach to teaching with *The Primary Comprehension Toolkit* in the primary grades was somewhat different than in the intermediate grades. Rather than building a curriculum framework around comprehension strategies, we let the basal series provide the structure. Unlike text selections in the intermediate grades, the primary basal reading selections are sequenced from easier to more difficult, and there is a clear progression of text difficulty and sophistication. Equally important, the phonemic awareness and phonics skills, high-frequency words, and word work are correlated with the selections, and these clearly needed to proceed in order. We did not feel comfortable rearranging the sequence of basal materials in kindergarten and first grade as we had for the upper grades.

We decided, then, to teach *Toolkit* lessons—primarily with the materials in the *Toolkits* and an occasional additional trade book—on the day each week that the basal set aside for review. This way, we reasoned, the students could begin to benefit from the *Toolkit* approach to using strategies, and we could avoid interrupting the flow of other important skills for early reading. Teachers then integrated the strategy that had been taught on the review day wherever possible in the following week or future weeks. They took advantage of many opportunities: independent reading, appropriate selections from the basal, and especially science and social studies lessons (where the strategies greatly benefited students in learning content).

We discovered that a Post-it and a nonfiction book with provocative pictures are powerful things in the hands of a five- or six-year-old. Students who could not yet read the words on the page or write them independently drew detailed representations of what they were learning—like eight carefully made circles for a spider's legs. Children used whatever inventive spelling they could—or enlisted a teacher's scribing help—to express a multitude of questions: "Why do they have a long tail?" "What does the pig eat?" "Why is the bat hanging upside down?" They also, without prompting, copied words from the texts to label their pictures, getting practice in forming letters and writing words they had not yet been exposed to, and they spontaneously shared what they were noticing with their classmates. Children also became more and more independent in spending productive time with texts. In fact, we recognized that sometimes the kindergartners, who could not read the texts, spent more time delving deeply into the pictures and therefore came

*Toolkit* practices affect independent work and small-group instruction.

up with more developed questions and inferences than the first graders who focused on the very simple words ("This is a fish,"or "This is a shark"). We wondered if, in our determination to teach kids to break the code, we were also breaking them of lingering on all the other rich sources of learning in nonfiction.

This thinking led us also to reexamine how we teach comprehension in our daily small-group guided reading lessons. We use a two-day lesson plan. The first day begins with rereading a familiar text and then moves to introduction, reading, and discussion of a new book. The second day, children reread the new book, do word work, and write. Typically, our "comprehension" discussions set children up for later writing and tended to be very short assessments of whether children had understood basic concepts in the book and made connections to their lives. For example:

Teacher: The animals ate a lot of different foods. What is your favorite food?
Student: I like pizza.

However, when we saw how deeply children could delve into information when they asked their own questions and made inferences from the pictures as well as the text, we began to incorporate these discussions into the after-reading portion of all our lessons. The conversation changed:

Teacher: What are you thinking about on these pages?
Student 1: I wonder if the mother gets food for her baby.
Student 2: Maybe she hides in the river to surprise her prey.

We are still in the process of trying to develop this approach, which has the potential to lead to much richer use of vocabulary, academic language, and thinking. Rather than limit children by what they can currently decode and our preconceived notions of what they should understand, these discussions open up great possibilities for young learners at any stage of reading development.

## Sustaining the Focus on Good Teaching

Developing ways to integrate and adapt new materials and approaches is one thing, but keeping enthusiasm, dedication, and creative teaching going across the years is another. Some teachers have belief systems about teaching that are totally aligned with the *Toolkits*. These teachers take to the approach quickly and with great enthusiasm, bringing out the brilliance in their students. They view teaching as an endlessly challenging puzzle and are fully engaged in fitting the pieces together. The *Toolkits* are not a program or prescription to these teachers; the *Toolkits* are a tool to help them unlock that puzzle. Not all teachers are equally open. Some have settled into a teacher-directed recitation mode and may be reluctant to spend the time to plan more student-centered, reflective lessons. Others may be open to active literacy but lack a variety of understandings about teaching strategies, about the meaning of thinking aloud, or about the teaching steps in a gradual release lesson. Our goal is to nurture—over time—a collegial environment in which all these teachers learn from the *Toolkit* approach. We believe that a sustained effort requires three essential ingredients: school administrators who support the work; professional development that engages, informs, and inspires educators; and thoughtful assessment and reflection that consider the results.

### Administrative Support

Principals, of course, set the tone for everything that happens in a school. Since our project began as a pilot, we have included schools based on their principals' choice to join. Often they have "signed up" because the teachers and administrators visited *Toolkit* schools and liked what they saw or because they attended workshops that introduced the *Toolkits* and answered their questions. We rely on our principals to provide the time for instruction and collaborative planning and to facilitate—either personally or by setting expectations—the ongoing environment and professional conversations that solve problems and maintain the focus and integrity of the work.

To help administrators support and monitor *Toolkit* implementation, we developed a short set of "look fors" that break down each section of the gradual release of responsibility in the lesson. We laid out explicitly what to look for when observing a successful *Toolkit* classroom. We started with a section about classroom environment and included attributes such as anchor charts and a gathering place. We specified desired teacher behaviors like "encouragement of risk-taking in student thinking (e.g., honoring varied responses, probing for depth)." We described what they should be seeing in each section of the *Toolkit* lesson. For Connect & Engage, for example, we included, "Teacher activates and assesses prior knowledge, including vocabulary and concepts, as needed, in brief, focused introduction," and "Teacher introduces strategy(ies), including purpose." In addition to aiding principals, this tool has been used by teachers and coaches to observe and discuss instruction. It has also helped us to meet Title I regulations for monitoring and to provide data on areas of strength and weakness across the project. These results, in turn, help us plan professional development opportunities.

> We dedicate ourselves to mutual support, observation, reflection, and ongoing professional learning.

### Professional Development

Support is essential. The *Toolkits* themselves, especially the Teacher's Guide and the video clips on the CD-ROM or DVD-ROM, offer a lot of information on implementation. But as this book notes, the *Toolkits* represent a paradigm shift for many teachers—from the proverbial "sage on the stage" to "guide on the side"—and seeing someone teach or having someone guide the planning process or working with someone to set up the physical space of a classroom is invaluable. Since our district has added schools and classes within schools in stages over five years, professional development needs to look different for different teachers. While many factors may be beyond our direct control, we believe that, like all learners, every teacher advances when supported in his or her zone of proximal development. It is our job to recognize where that is for each teacher and to scaffold the next steps along the way to making the use of the *Toolkits* more meaningful and effective in every classroom.

The following professional development practices illustrate how some of the ideas and practices discussed in this book can be incorporated into a district staff development plan:

- **Where possible, teachers have participated in a book study of *Strategies That Work* prior to starting *Toolkits*.** Having time to learn the thinking behind comprehension strategy instruction in general and behind each strategy in particular gives teachers background knowledge and a common language.

- **An introductory workshop, ideally conducted before the school year begins, gives teachers new to *Toolkits* a head start.** Beginning a new school year *and* a new approach can be overwhelming. A general overview of the philosophy, approach, and parts of the *Toolkits* (see the PowerPoint presentations on the *Staff Development Resources* CD-ROM) can demystify the process.

- **Grade-level workshops or study groups at the beginning of each unit encourage teachers to think about the purpose of each lesson and how the lessons in each strategy book fit together.** This establishes a clear overall picture of where the work is going and why.

- **Providing time for collaborative planning and showing teachers how to do it allow us to explore together the many decisions that make a lesson successful.** We use a lesson template based on the gradual release steps in the *Toolkits* to plan lessons with teachers, encouraging them to adjust their lessons to meet the needs of the specific students and the teachers' own authentic thinking. We advocate strongly for collaborative planning because it lets teachers into each other's heads to enrich the process of constructing a lesson and because collaboration builds trust and rapport among colleagues.

- **Demonstration lessons help teachers experience and understand what an active literacy classroom looks and sounds like.** No method is as effective as the demonstration lesson to capture the complexity of the interactions and the moment-to-moment decisions that occur in every lesson. We have included special educators and ELL teachers in both teaching and viewing demonstration lessons, which enriches everyone's understanding of how to differentiate for specific student needs. We find that the common language of the *Toolkits* helps us talk with one another to improve our practice. We have also created videotapes of our teachers and posted them on internal websites to support ongoing discussion of best practices.

- **Workshops focused on specific areas solve problems, enhance practice, or both.** After identifying areas of common need or interest—conferring, analyzing student work, integrating strategy instruction in content areas, working with ELLs, and the like— a coach or reading specialist leads a workshop, sometimes teaching in a single school and sometimes teaching in several schools brought together.

- **A *Toolkit* inquiry group moves everyone forward.** To reach and sustain high-level work in a large school system like ours, it's critical that we have a strong cadre of teachers who are committed to working and to constantly broadening their expertise. We have convened an inquiry group composed of many of our lead *Toolkit* teachers several times across the school year to address issues such as the ways to assign grades in *Toolkit* classrooms, the relationship of our teaching to the state tests, and the needed curriculum revisions. This inquiry group provides the district with a wealth of knowledge to move our work forward and has become a professional learning community that energizes and inspires the teachers involved.

## Assessment of Progress

We have consistently surveyed our teachers, through written feedback and workshops and focus-group meetings, to learn their reactions to the *Toolkits*. They often comment on the changes in their own teaching:

"I have learned to not always expect a specific answer. I have opened the classroom to allow the students' thinking and interests to guide the lessons."

"I listen more to what my students have to say."

"I communicate more with my students; I have more patience."

"Wow! I learned how to teach THINKING!"

These teaching behaviors translate into student behaviors that the teachers note:

"I believe my classroom is more of a community."

"A big change in motivation to read, confidence, taking risks, and expansion of thinking!"

"They seem more interested in reading—they feel they 'own' the work more than before."

"My students are more polite and are learning to listen to each other more often."

"[I notice] the talking of the below grade level readers—their confidence and participation now in small-group instruction."

Finally, teachers express how these changes in classroom environment allow for higher levels of learning:

"Students are able to verbalize connections, learn from each other, and understand more fully."

"My students are more active readers. They are able to read more critically and have deeper discussions."

"They are more reflective when responding."

"The children were actually thinking about what they were reading."

Test scores soared dramatically in many classrooms. In one school with 84 percent Free and Reduced Meal (FARM) students and 55 percent ELLs that has fully embraced the *Toolkits*, 97 percent of the fifth graders scored proficient or advanced on the state reading test in 2009. In another school with 73 percent FARMs and 35 percent ELLs, 92 percent of the fifth graders were proficient or advanced.

Still, the *Toolkits* are not a magic bullet or a quick fix. Several *Toolkit* schools are still not making Adequate Yearly Progress (AYP). As everywhere else, many factors impact test scores and instruction: Do teachers have sufficient time to teach reading? Is collaborative planning time scheduled and used effectively? Does the climate of the school promote engagement, higher-order thinking, and rigor? A "no" answer to any one of these questions casts a shadow across the landscape of learning.

Nevertheless, we have volumes of anecdotal evidence of the growth of our children's thinking in classrooms that have brought to life the principles of active literacy from the *Toolkits*. I will always remember a day early in the year in a fifth grade classroom where the students had a reputation for being hard to engage. They had just begun work with the *Toolkits*. Kids were sprawled out on the carpet, working on one of the *Toolkit* lessons, and one boy exclaimed, "This is hard. But it's sure interesting!" You could see on his face puzzlement at the notion that "hard" could actually be a good thing, a challenge that stimulates the intellect rather than an obstacle that needs to be avoided. Another time at a workshop, a teacher shared a collection of the comic strips that one of her special education students had created on Post-its. He had difficulty writing, so he took to making incredibly detailed comic strips to leave tracks of his thinking. He had become something of a hero to the other students, who routinely asked him to share his work.

We've watched students who are just beginning to speak English volunteer their thinking and take their time trying to express themselves to the whole class, knowing that theirs is a classroom that honors their ideas as much as anyone else's and will give them time to articulate them. The growth in literacy, particularly among these ELLs, has been obvious, as they have been given constant opportunities to rehearse their thinking during turn and talk as well as to practice their academic language orally and in written notes.

There are also many opportunities to celebrate the thinking of children who cannot yet express themselves in English, incorporating drawing and working in groups with bilingual classmates who speak their language. A fifth grade boy who had recently arrived in this country and spoke only Spanish worked on a group poster about the poem "Asteroids" by Myra Cohn Livingston. He wrote in Spanish what his classmate then translated: "The poet wants to compare the asteroids to some soccer players, but the difference is that the asteroids never stop moving."

We have also seen the *Toolkits* challenge above-grade-level readers. One girl who always scored high on reading tests had difficulty writing her thoughts in the response column of her F/Q/R chart. She was so used to feeding back what the teacher wanted to hear that she didn't know how to make an authentic personal response to her reading. Moving her out of her comfort zone of "the right answer" opened up a whole new understanding of what it means to be a strong reader and steered her toward much higher levels of analytical thinking.

## New Challenges

A good deal of our attention goes to supporting schools where teachers are new to the *Toolkits* or where they may not have fully implemented them or have questions about how to do so. At the same time, we always consider how to move our overall work forward. We are particularly interested in how to emphasize flexible use of strategies and strategies as means rather than ends. We see as the goal of *Toolkit* work not to have our students write three text-to-self connections on a worksheet but to have them use strategies as a bridge to higher levels of thinking, understanding, and impacting their world. One way we are approaching this goal is by creating units that focus on a topic and pacing our strategies as they help children develop their thinking about the topic. This year's *Toolkit* Inquiry Group worked in grade-level groups to design units around topics they chose that related to their science and social studies curriculums, including habitats, immigration, and the American Revolution. By reading multiple texts on various aspects of a topic, students build a body of knowledge and experience different perspectives that allow their discussions and analysis to go far deeper. Moving into the era of Common Core State Standards, we see how our *Toolkit* work on these integrated units can lead the way.

Five years ago, we planted the seeds of our *Toolkit* work; today, we are reaping many benefits. It takes work, keeping our intentions from being overrun by the weeds of old habits and easier paths. But every day we see students who are more engaged in reading, who know that their thinking matters, and who therefore think harder and more about their reading. We see students like the first grader who drew a girl in the middle of mounds of books in the library as her visualization of a story read by her teacher. She wrote in invented spelling on her Post-it: "I saw a gorle going to the libiary. And she brod books. She just cont not get a nuf." (I saw a girl going to the library. And she borrowed books. She just could not get enough.") We have seen so many students who have learned that when it comes to reading and thinking, they just can't get enough. That is the sweet fruit of our labor.

# Appendix A: Contents of the *Staff Development Resources* CD-ROM

## Handouts and PowerPoints

| Chapter | Resource |
|---------|----------|
| 1 – Comprehension Strategies | • "Celebration of the Human Voice" by Eduardo Galeano<br>• "Using Comprehension Strategies" thinksheet<br>• Common Core Reading Standards and *Toolkit* correlation charts |
| 2 – Active Literacy | • "Active Literacy Viewing Guide"<br>• "How Do We Create an Active Literacy Classroom?" from *The Comprehension Toolkit* Teacher's Guide, pages 13-18 |
| 3 – Text Selection | • "Text Talk" presentation template |
| 4 – Gradual Release of Responsibility and Conferring | • "Gradual Release of Responsibility Note-Taking Grid"<br>• "Gradual Release of Responsibility Viewing Guide"<br>• List titled "Suggested Conferences to Analyze"<br>• "Conferring Considerations"<br>• "Gradual Release of Responsibility Lesson Planning"<br>• "Reading Comprehension: What Works?" *Educational Leadership* 51,5: 62-67 by Linda Fielding and P. David Pearson<br>• "Independent Reading Conference Form" |
| 5 – Modeling: Think-Alouds and Demonstrations | • "Secrets" from *The Comprehension Toolkit, Source Book of Short Texts*, page 37<br>• "Steps for Creating a Think-Aloud"<br>• "Think Aloud, Modeling the Cognitive Processes of Reading Comprehension" in the *Journal of Reading* 27:44-47 (1983) by Beth Davey |
| 6 – Assessment and Evaluation | • Copy of Lesson 1, "Follow Your Inner Conversation," in strategy book 1: *Monitor Comprehension*, pages 2-11 from *The Comprehension Toolkit*<br>• Copy of "Annotated Rubric for Strategy Cluster 1," strategy book 1: *Monitor Comprehension*, page 40 from *The Comprehension Toolkit* |

| Chapter | Resource |
|---|---|
| 6 – Assessment and Evaluation *(continued)* | • Copy of Lesson 5, "Merge Thinking with New Learning," in strategy book 2, *Activate & Connect*, pages 14-25 from *The Comprehension Toolkit*<br><br>• Copy of "Annotated Rubric for Strategy Cluster 2," strategy book 2, *Activate & Connect*, page 40 from *The Comprehension Toolkit*<br><br>• Assessing While Teaching chart |
| 7 – Content Literacy Across the Curriculum | • Two-column chart: "Observations" and "Questions"<br><br>• Copy of "Hallmarks for Creating an Environment for Thoughtful Content Literacy Instruction"<br><br>• Copy of the content literacy section from *The Comprehension Toolkit, Extend & Investigate*, pages 8–22<br><br>• Chapter 8, "History Lessons," by Anne Goudvis and Brad Buhrow<br><br>• Chapter 9, "Comprehension in Science," by Gina Cervetti from *Comprehension Going Forward*<br><br>• Chapter 12, "Reading for Understanding in Social Studies and Science" from *Strategies That Work*<br><br>• Content Literacy Monitoring Sheet |
| PowerPoint Presentations and Handouts | • Giving an Overview: *The Comprehension Toolkit* and *The Primary Comprehension Toolkit*<br><br>• Introducing *The Primary Comprehension Toolkit: Language and Lessons for Active Literacy*<br><br>• Introducing *The Comprehension Toolkit: Language and Lessons for Active Literacy*<br><br>• Presentation Handouts |

Correlation to Stephanie Harvey & Anne Goudvis'

## *The Primary Comprehension Toolkit*
Grades K–2

## *The Comprehension Toolkit*
Grades 3–6

# Common Core Standards: Reading Standards for Informational Text Correlation to *The Primary Comprehension Toolkit, Grades K–2*

## Kindergarten

| Common Core Reading Standards for Informational Text | The Primary Comprehension Toolkit, Grades K–2 |
|---|---|
| **Key Ideas and Details** | |
| 1. With prompting and support, ask and answer questions about key details in a text. | LESSON 8 — View and Read to Learn and Wonder: Use images and words to gain understanding<br>LESSON 9 — Wonder about New Information: Ask questions when you read, listen and view |
| 2. With prompting and support, identify the main topic and retell key details of a text. | LESSON 16—Figure Out What's Important: Separate important information from interesting details. |
| 3. With prompting and support, describe the connection between two individuals, events, ideas, or pieces of information in a text. | LESSON 6— Make Connections: Use personal experience to construct meaning |
| **Craft and Structure** | |
| 4. With prompting and support, ask and answer questions about unknown words in a text | LESSON 12—Infer Meaning: Merge Background Knowledge with Clues from the Text |
| 5. Identify the front cover, back cover, and title page of a book. | LESSON 2— Notice and Think about Nonfiction Features: Construct a Feature/Purpose chart |
| **Integration of Knowledge and Ideas** | |
| 7. With prompting and support, describe the relationship between illustrations and the text in which they appear (e.g., what person, place, thing, or idea in the text an illustration depicts). | LESSON 14—Make Sense of New Information: Infer from features, pictures and words |

# Common Core Standards: Reading Standards for Informational Text Correlation to *The Primary Comprehension Toolkit*, Grades K–2

## Kindergarten

| Common Core Reading Standards for Informational Text | The Primary Comprehension Toolkit, Grades K–2 |
| --- | --- |
| **Range of Reading and Level of Text Complexity** | |
| 10. Actively engage in group reading activities with purpose and understanding. | Every *Primary Comprehension Toolkit* lesson is organized around whole-group instruction that involves students in shared reading and text analysis. This is supported by the lesson text which are offered in an expansive poster format that lends itself to group analysis. Additional nonfiction texts are provided in a reproducible format that support students in collaborative reading and learning. |

# Common Core Standards: Reading Standards for Informational Text Correlation to *The Primary Comprehension Toolkit*, Grades K–2

## Grade 1

| Common Core Reading Standards for Informational Text | The Primary Comprehension Toolkit, Grades K–2 |
|---|---|
| **Key Ideas and Details** | |
| 1. Ask and answer questions about key details in a text. | LESSON 8 — View and Read to Learn and Wonder: Use Images and words to gain understanding<br>LESSON 9 — Wonder about New Information: Ask questions when you read, listen and view<br>LESSON 10 — Use Questions as Tools for Learning; Understand why some questions are answered and some are not |
| 2. Identify the main topic and retell key details of a text. | LESSON 16 — Figure Out What's Important: Separate important information from interesting details.<br>LESSON 17 — Paraphrase Information: Merge your thinking to make meaning |
| 3. Describe the connection between two individuals, events, ideas, or pieces of information in a text. | LESSON 6 — Make Connections: Use personal experience to construct meaning |
| **Craft and Structure** | |
| 4. Ask and answer questions to help determine or clarify the meaning of words and phrases in a text. | LESSON 8 — View and Read to Learn and Wonder: Use images and words to gain understanding |
| 5. Know and use various text features (e.g., headings, tables of contents, glossaries, electronic menus, icons) to locate key facts or information in a text. | LESSON 2 — Notice and Think about Nonfiction Features: Construct a Feature/Purpose chart<br>LESSON 3 — Explore Nonfiction Features: Create Nonfiction Feature books |
| 6. Distinguish between information provided by pictures or other illustrations and information provided by the words in a text. | LESSON 14 — Make Sense of New Information: Infer from features, pictures and words |

# Common Core Standards: Reading Standards for Informational Text Correlation to *The Primary Comprehension Toolkit*, Grades K–2

## Grade 1

| Common Core Reading Standards for Informational Text | The Primary Comprehension Toolkit, Grades K–2 |
| --- | --- |
| **Integration of Knowledge and Ideas** | |
| 7. Use the illustrations and details in a text to describe its key ideas. | LESSON 19 —Summarize Information: Put it in your own words and keep it interesting<br><br>LESSON 20 —Read to Get the Big Ideas: Synthesize the text |
| 8. Identify the reasons an author gives to support points in a text. | LESSON 20 —Read to Get the Big Ideas: Synthesize the Text |
| **Range of Reading and Level of Text Complexity** | |
| 10. With prompting and support, read informational texts appropriately complex for grade 1. | To support guided reading and independent practice, *The Comprehension Toolkit* series offers age-appropriate informational text of increasing complexity. The *Source Book of Short Text* offers 39 short informational articles on a range of real-world science and social studies topics in English and Spanish. The PreK–Grade 1 *Toolkit Texts* resource book provides 40 cross-curricular articles in English and Spanish. |

# Common Core Standards: Reading Standards for Informational Text Correlation to *The Primary Comprehension Toolkit*, Grades K–2

## Grade 2

| Common Core Reading Standards for Informational Text | *The Primary Comprehension Toolkit*, Grades K–2 |
|---|---|
| **Key Ideas and Details** | |
| 1. Ask and answer such questions as *who, what, where, when, why,* and *how* to demonstrate understanding of key details in a text. | LESSON 9 — Wonder about New Information: Ask questions when you read, listen and view<br>LESSON 10 — Use Questions as Tools for Learning; Understand why some questions are answered and some are not<br>LESSON 11 — Read with a Question in Mind: Find Answers to Expand Thinking |
| 2. Identify the main topic of a multiparagraph text as well as the focus of specific paragraphs within the text. | LESSON 16 — Figure Out What's Important: Separate important information from interesting details. |
| **Craft and Structure** | |
| 4. Determine the meaning of words and phrases in a text relevant to a grade 2 topic or subject area. | LESSON 12 — Infer Meaning: Merge background knowledge with clues from the text |
| 5. Know and use various text features (e.g., captions, bold print, subheadings, glossaries, indexes, electronic menus, icons) to locate key facts or information in a text efficiently. | LESSON 2 — Notice and Think about Nonfiction Features: Construct a Feature/Purpose chart<br>LESSON 3 — Explore Nonfiction Features: Create Nonfiction Feature books |
| 6. Identify the main purpose of a text, including what the author wants to answer, explain, or describe. | LESSON 17 — Paraphrase Information: Merge your thinking to make meaning<br>LESSON 18 — Organize Your Thinking as You Read: Take notes to record information<br>LESSON 19 — Summarize Information: Put it in your own words and keep it interesting |

# Common Core Standards: Reading Standards for Informational Text Correlation to *The Primary Comprehension Toolkit*, Grades K–2

## Grade 2

| Common Core Reading Standards for Informational Text | *The Primary Comprehension Toolkit*, Grades K–2 |
|---|---|
| **Integration of Knowledge and Ideas** | |
| 7. Explain how specific images (e.g., a diagram showing how a machine works) contribute to and clarify a text. | LESSON 14 —Make Sense of New Information: Infer from features, pictures and words |
| 8. Describe how reasons support specific points the author makes in a text. | LESSON 20 —Read to Get the Big Ideas: Synthesize the text |
| **Range of Reading and Level of Text Complexity** | |
| 10. By the end of year, read and comprehend informational texts, including history/social studies, science, and technical texts, in the grades 2–3 text complexity band proficiently, with scaffolding as needed at the high end of the range. | To support guided reading and independent practice, *The Comprehension Toolkit* series offers age-appropriate informational text of increasing complexity. The *Source Book of Short Text* offers 39 short informational articles on a range of real-world science and social studies topics in English and Spanish. The *Toolkit Texts* resource books provide cross-curricular articles in English and Spanish. |

# Common Core Standards: Reading Standards for Informational Text Correlation to *The Comprehension Toolkit, Grades 3–6*

## Grade 3

| Common Core Reading Standards for Informational Text | The Comprehension Toolkit, Grades 3–6 |
|---|---|
| **Key Ideas and Details** | |
| 1. Ask and answer questions to demonstrate understanding of a text, referring explicitly to the text as the basis for the answers. | LESSON 7 — Question the Text: Learn to ask questions as you read<br>LESSON 8 — Read to Discover Answers: Ask questions to gain information<br>LESSON 9 — Ask Questions to Expand Thinking: Wonder about the text to understand the big ideas<br>LESSON 14—Read with a Question in Mind: Infer to answer your questions<br>*Extend and Investigate,* LESSON 4—Monitoring and Asking Questions When There is Not Enough Information (NEI) |
| 2. Determine the main idea of a text; recount the key details and explain how they support the main idea. | LESSON 18—Target Key Information: Code the text to hold thinking<br>LESSON 19—Determine What to Remember: Separate interesting details from important ideas<br>LESSON 21—Construct Main Ideas from Supporting Details: Create a Topic/Detail/Response chart |
| **Craft and Structure** | |
| 4. Determine the meaning of general academic words and domain-specific words and phrases in a text relevant to *a grade 3 topic or subject area.* | LESSON 10—Infer the Meaning of Unfamiliar Words: Use context clues to unpack vocabulary<br>LESSON 12—Tackle the Meaning of Language: Infer beyond the literal meaning<br>*Extend and Investigate,* LESSON 7—Unpacking New Words and Concepts |
| 5. Use text features and search tools (e.g. key words, sidebars, hyperlinks) to locate information relevant to a given topic efficiently. | LESSON 4 — Follow the Text Signposts: Use nonfiction features to guide learning<br>LESSON 13—Crack Open Features: Infer the meaning of subheads and titles<br>*Extend and Investigate,* LESSON 10—Drawing Conclusions from Graphic Features |
| 6. Distinguish their own point of view from that of the author of a text. | LESSON 20—Distinguish Your Thinking from the Author's: Contrast what you think with the author's perspective |

# Common Core Standards: Reading Standards for Informational Text Correlation to *The Comprehension Toolkit*, Grades 3–6

| Common Core Reading Standards for Informational Text | *The Comprehension Toolkit*, Grades 3–6 |
|---|---|
| **Integration of Knowledge and Ideas** | |
| 7. Use information gained from illustrations (e.g. maps, photographs) and the words in a text to demonstrate understanding of the text (e.g. where, when, why, and how key events occur). | LESSON 4 — Follow the Text Signposts: Use nonfiction features to guide learning |
| 8. Describe the logical connection between particular sentences and paragraphs in a text (e.g. comparison, cause/effect, first/second/third in a sequence). | LESSON 11 —Infer with Text Clues: Draw conclusions from text evidence |
| 9. Compare and contrast most important points and key details presented in two texts on the same topic. | LESSON 23 — Think Beyond the Text: Move from facts to ideas<br>LESSON 24 — Read to Get the Gist: Synthesize your thinking as you go |
| **Range of Reading and Level of Text Complexity** | |
| 10. By the end of the year, read and comprehend informational texts, including history/social studies, science, and technical texts, at the high end of the grades 2–3 text complexity band independently and proficiently. | To support guided reading and independent practice, *The Comprehension Toolkit* series offers a range of informational text of increasing complexity. The *Source Book of Short Text* offers 43 short informational articles on a range of real-world science and social studies topics. *Extend and Investigate* offers units of study on content area reading and research, textbook reading, and test reading. The *Toolkit Texts* resource books provide cross-curricular articles in English and Spanish. |

# Common Core Standards: Reading Standards for Informational Text Correlation to *The Comprehension Toolkit*, Grades 3–6

## Grade 4

| Common Core Reading Standards for Informational Text | The Comprehension Toolkit, Grades 3–6 |
|---|---|
| **Key Ideas and Details** | |
| 1. Refer to details and examples in a text when explaining what the text says explicitly and when drawing inferences from the text. | LESSON 11—Infer with Text Clues: Draw conclusions from text evidence. |
| 2. Determine the main idea of a text and explain how it is supported by key details; summarize the text. | LESSON 21—Construct Main Ideas from Supporting Details: Create a Topic/Detail/Response chart<br>LESSON 24—Read to Get the Gist: Synthesize your thinking as you go<br>*Extend and Investigate*, LESSON 2—Topic/Detail Notetaking |
| **Craft and Structure** | |
| 4. Determine the meaning of general academic and domain-specific words or phrases in a text relevant to *a grade 4 topic or subject area.* | LESSON 10—Infer the Meaning of Unfamiliar Words: Use context clues to unpack vocabulary |
| **Integration of Knowledge and Ideas** | |
| 7. Interpret information presented visually, orally, or quantitatively (e.g., in charts, graphs, diagrams, time lines, animations, or interactive elements on Web pages) and explain how the information contributes to an understanding of the text in which it appears. | LESSON 4—Follow the Text Sign Posts: Use nonfiction features to guide learning<br>LESSON 13—Crack Open Features: Infer the meaning of subheads and titles<br>*Extend and Investigate*, LESSON 3—Getting to the Point |
| 8. Explain how an author uses reasons and evidence to support particular points in a text. | LESSON 15—Wrap your Mind Around the Big Ideas: Use text evidence to infer themes |
| 9. Integrate information from two texts on the same topic in order to write or speak about the subject knowledgeably. | LESSON 22—Read, Think and React: Paraphrase and respond to information |

# Common Core Standards: Reading Standards for Informational Text Correlation to *The Comprehension Toolkit*, Grades 3–6

| Common Core Reading Standards for Informational Text | *The Comprehension Toolkit*, Grades 3–6 |
|---|---|
| **Range of Reading and Level of Text Complexity** | |
| 10. **By the end of year, read and comprehend informational texts, including history/social studies, science, and technical texts, in the grades 4–5 text complexity band proficiently, with scaffolding as needed at the high end of the range.** | To support guided reading and independent practice, *The Comprehension Toolkit* series offers a range of informational text of increasing complexity. The *Source Book of Short Text* offers 43 short informational articles on a range of real-world science and social studies topics. *Extend and Investigate* offers units of study on content area reading and research, textbook reading, and test reading. The *Toolkit Texts* resource books provide cross-curricular articles in English and Spanish. |

# Common Core Standards: Reading Standards for Informational Text Correlation to *The Comprehension Toolkit*, Grades 3–6

## Grade 5

| Common Core Reading Standards for Informational Text | *The Comprehension Toolkit*, Grades 3–6 |
|---|---|
| **Key Ideas and Details** | |
| 1. Quote accurately from a text when explaining what the text says explicitly and when drawing inferences from the text. | LESSON 11—Infer with Text Clues: Draw conclusions from text evidence<br>LESSON 15—Wrap Your Mind Around the Big Ideas: Use text evidence to infer themes |
| 2. Determine two or more main ideas of a text and explain how they are supported by key details; summarize the text. | LESSON 18—Target Key Information: Code the text to hold thinking<br>LESSON 19—Determine What To Remember: Separate interesting details from important ideas |
| **Craft and Structure** | |
| 4. Determine the meaning of general academic and domain-specific words and phrases in a text relevant to a *grade 5 topic or subject area*. | LESSON 10—Infer the Meaning of Unfamiliar Words: Use context clues to unpack vocabulary |
| **Integration of Knowledge and Ideas** | |
| 7. Draw on information from multiple print or digital sources, demonstrating the ability to locate an answer to a question quickly or to solve a problem efficiently. | LESSON 8 — Read to Discover Answers: Ask questions to gain information<br>LESSON 14—Read with a Question in Mind: Infer to answer your questions |
| 8. Explain how an author uses reasons and evidence to support particular points in a text, identifying which reasons and evidence support which point(s). | LESSON 11—Infer with Text Clues:  Draw conclusions from text evidence |
| **Range of Reading and Level of Text Complexity** | |
| 10. By the end of the year, read and comprehend informational texts, including history/social studies, science, and technical texts, at the high end of the grades 4–5 text complexity band independently and proficiently. | To support guided reading and independent practice, *The Comprehension Toolkit* series offers a range of informational text of increasing complexity. The *Source Book of Short Text* offers 43 short informational articles on a range of real-world science and social studies topics. *Extend and Investigate* offers units of study on content area reading and research, textbook reading, and test reading. The *Toolkit Texts* resource books provide cross-curricular articles in English and Spanish. |

## Common Core Standards: Reading Standards for Informational Text Correlation to *The Comprehension Toolkit*, Grades 3–6

## Grade 6

| Common Core Reading Standards for Informational Text | The Comprehension Toolkit, Grades 3–6 |
|---|---|
| **Key Ideas and Details** | |
| 1. Cite textual evidence to support analysis of what the text says explicitly as well as inferences drawn from the text. | LESSON 11—Infer with Text Clues: Draw conclusions from text evidence<br>LESSON 15—Wrap Your Mind Around the Big Ideas: Use text evidence to infer themes |
| 2. Determine a central idea of a text and how it is conveyed through particular details; provide a summary of the text distinct from personal opinions or judgments. | LESSON 18—Target Key Information: Code the text to hold thinking<br>LESSON 19—Determine What to Remember: Separate interesting details from important ideas<br>LESSON 25—Reread and Rethink: Rethink misconceptions and tie opinions to the text<br>*Extend and Investigate*, LESSON 2—Topic/Detail Notetaking |
| 3. Analyze in detail how a key individual, event, or idea is introduced, illustrated, and elaborated in a text (e.g., through examples or anecdotes). | LESSON 23—Think Beyond the Text: Move from facts to ideas<br>LESSON 24—Read to Get The Gist: Synthesize your thinking as you go |
| **Craft and Structure** | |
| 4. Determine the meaning of words and phrases as they are used in a text, including figurative, connotative, and technical meanings. | LESSON 12—Tackle the Meaning of Language: Infer beyond the literal meaning<br>*Extend and Investigate*, LESSON 7—Unpacking New Words and Concepts |
| 6. Determine an author's point of view or purpose in a text and explain how it is conveyed in the text. | LESSON 20—Distinguish Your Thinking from the Author's: Contrast what you think with the author's perspective<br>*Extend and Investigate*, LESSON 3— Getting to the Point |
| **Integration of Knowledge and Ideas** | |
| 7. Integrate information presented in different media or formats (e.g., visually, quantitatively) as well as in words to develop a coherent understanding of a topic or issue. | *Extend and Investigate*, LESSON 10—Drawing Conclusions from Graphic Features |

# Common Core Standards: Reading Standards for Informational Text Correlation to *The Comprehension Toolkit*, Grades 3–6

| Common Core Reading Standards for Informational Text | *The Comprehension Toolkit*, Grades 3–6 |
| --- | --- |
| **Integration of Knowledge and Ideas, con't.** | |
| 8. Trace and evaluate the argument and specific claims in a text, distinguishing claims that are supported by reasons and evidence from claims that are not. | LESSON 11—Infer with Text Clues: Draw conclusions from text evidence |
| **Range of Reading and Level of Text Complexity** | |
| 10. By the end of the year, read and comprehend literary nonfiction in the grades 6–8 text complexity band proficiently, with scaffolding as needed at the high end of the range. | To support guided reading and independent practice, *The Comprehension Toolkit* series offers a range of informational text of increasing complexity. *The Source Book of Short Text* offers 43 short informational articles on a range of real-world science and social studies topics. *Extend and Investigate* offers units of study on content area reading and research, textbook reading, and test reading. The *Toolkit Texts* resource books provide cross-curricular articles in English and Spanish. |

## Addendum to Common Core State Standards and *Toolkits* Correlation Charts

In addition to being perfectly aligned with the Common Core State Standards (CCSS) for reading informational texts, the *Toolkits'* practices and components also support you in addressing the writing, speaking and listening, and language standards.

### Writing Standards

Like the CCSS, *The Comprehension Toolkit* series adheres to an integrated approach to literacy. Reading, writing, speaking, and listening are interconnected in each lesson. Students are regularly required to record the tracks of their thinking and to chart their learning as they read a nonfiction text. In the Reflection & Assessment section of each lesson, students demonstrate their learning and understanding through a variety of written and oral responses. These responses involve students in drawing evidence from informational texts and writing informative/explanatory texts that examine and convey complex ideas and information clearly and accurately.

Harvey Daniels and Stephanie Harvey's comprehensive guide to cross-curricular projects, *Comprehension and Collaboration*, describes how to coach students through the entire research to presentation process. In addition to writing a range of informative/explanatory texts, students also explore different ways for sharing their findings and beliefs with others.

### Speaking and Listening Standards

Through its active literacy instruction, *The Comprehension Toolkit* series provides students with ample opportunities to take part in a variety of rich, structured conversations—as part of a whole class, in small groups, and with a partner. *Toolkit* lessons regularly require students to turn and talk with a partner; engage in collaborative group discussions; contribute accurate, relevant information; make comparisons and contrasts; and analyze and synthesize a multitude of ideas in various domains.

The small-group lessons in *Comprehension Intervention* reinforce and extend the *Toolkits'* collaborative comprehension instruction and support needs-based guided-reading groups and special education inclusion.

The previews and extensions in *Scaffolding the Comprehension Toolkit for English Language Learners* help English language learners actively participate in every *Toolkit* lesson and express what they fully comprehend.

*Comprehension and Collaboration* builds on the *Toolkits'* practices by providing how-to instructions for four types of inquiry circles and includes 26 practical lessons in comprehension, collaboration, and research. The companion *Inquiry Circles* DVDs show these inquiry circles in action and model how to teach strategic thinking and collaboration.

## Language Standards

Through its exploration of fundamental comprehension strategies, *Toolkit* lessons help students learn conventions of standard English; determine or clarify the meaning of grade-appropriate words encountered through listening, reading, and media use; come to appreciate that words have nonliteral meanings, shadings of meaning, and relationships to other words; and expand their vocabulary in the course of studying content.

The previews and extensions in *Scaffolding the Comprehension Toolkit for English Language Learners* guide students in unpacking the vocabulary and language structures in every *Toolkit* lesson.

The short nonfiction articles in the *Toolkit Texts* series introduce new vocabulary and build background knowledge in numerous content areas.

# Works Cited

Allington, Richard L. 2002. "What I've Learned About Effective Reading Instruction from a Decade of Studying Exemplary Elementary Classroom Teachers." *Phi Delta Kappan* 83 (June): 740-747.

Allington, Richard. 2008. *What Really Matters in Response to Intervention: Research-Based Designs*. Boston, Massachusetts: Allyn and Bacon, Inc.

Boreen, Jean, Mary K. Johnson, Donna Naday, and Joe Potts. 2000. *Mentoring Beginning Teachers*. Portland, Maine: Stenhouse.

Daniels, Harvey, and Stephanie Harvey. 2009. *Comprehension and Collaboration: Inquiry Circles in Action*. Portsmouth, New Hampshire: Heinemann.

Davey, Beth. 1983. "Think Aloud: Modeling the Cognitive Processes of Reading Comprehension." *Journal of Reading* 27:44–47.

Dozier, Cheryl. 2006. *Responsive Literacy Coaching*. Portland, Maine: Stenhouse.

Harvey, Stephanie and Anne Goudvis. 2007. *Strategies That Work: Teaching Comprehension for Understanding and Engagement*. Portland, Maine: Stenhouse.

Harvey, Stephanie, Anne Goudvis, and Judy Wallis. 2010. *Comprehension Intervention: Small-Group Lessons for The Comprehension Toolkit*. Portsmouth, New Hampshire: Heinemann.

Harvey, Stephanie, Anne Goudvis, and Judy Wallis. 2010. *Comprehension Intervention: Small-Group Lessons for The Primary Comprehension Toolkit*. Portsmouth, New Hampshire: Heinemann.

Hindley, Joanne. 1996. *In the Company of Children*. Portland, Maine: Stenhouse.

Keene, Ellin Oliver and Susan Zimmermann. 2007. *Mosaic of Thought*. Portsmouth, New Hampshire: Heinemann.

Keene, Ellin Oliver, Susan Zimmermann, Debbie Miller, Samantha Bennett, Leslie Blauman, Chryse Hutchins, Stephanie Harvey, et al. 2011. *Comprehension Going Forward: Where We Are and What's Next*. Portsmouth, New Hampshire: Heinemann.

Pearson, P. David, and M.C. Gallagher. 1983. "The Instruction of Reading Comprehension." *Contemporary Educational Psychology* 8:317–344.

Pearson, P. David, J.A. Dole, G.G. Duffy, and L.R. Roehler. 1992."Developing Expertise in Reading Comprehension: What Should Be Taught and How Should It Be Taught?" In *What Research Has to Say to the Teacher of Reading*, edited by J. Farstrup and S.J. Samuels. Newark, Delaware: International Reading Association.

Pressley, Michael. 2002. *Reading Instruction That Works: The Case for Balanced Teaching*, 2nd ed. New York: Guilford Press.

Serravallo, Jennifer, and Gravity Goldberg. 2007. *Conferring with Readers: Supporting Each Student's Growth and Independence*. Portsmouth, New Hampshire: Heinemann.

# Comprehension Intervention

*Small-Group Lessons for The Comprehension Toolkit Series*

*"We created* Comprehension Intervention *as a resource to provide additional support to kids who need more time and more explicit instruction to integrate comprehension strategies and use them as tools for learning and understanding."*

—STEPHANIE HARVEY, ANNE GOUDVIS & JUDY WALLIS

Created to follow each *Toolkit* lesson, the *Comprehension Intervention* small-group lessons narrow the instructional focus, concentrating on critical aspects of the *Toolkit's* lesson strategy to reinforce kids' understanding, step by step. Approaching each *Toolkit* strategy lesson in a new way with new texts, *Comprehension Intervention* lessons lend themselves to a variety of instructional settings:

■ By explicitly reinforcing and extending *Toolkit* lessons, these lessons are ideal for small, needs-based **guided-reading groups**.

■ In breaking down *Toolkit* instruction into smaller steps, these lessons make learning more accessible for students requiring **tier 2 RTI** instruction.

■ Infinitely flexible and targeted, these lessons help teachers increase instructional intensity, allowing additional time for **tier 3 RTI** instruction.

■ Based on shared readings, which allow for natural differentiation, the *Toolkit* whole-group lessons are ideal for **special-ed inclusion.** *Comprehension Intervention* lessons then offer additional targeted small-group follow-up interventions.

*To learn more or purchase, visit* **Heinemann.com**

DEDICATED TO TEACHERS™

*ideal for whiteboard analysis*

## Toolkit Texts
### Short Nonfiction for Guided and Independent Practice

*"These articles lend themselves to active reading, giving kids a great place to annotate and work out their thinking as they read."*

—STEPHANIE HARVEY & ANNE GOUDVIS

Recognizing that effective comprehension instruction begins with engaging texts, Steph and Anne developed the four-volume *Toolkit Texts* series. Each volume is a library of short nonfiction articles in a reproducible format

■ Articles focus on **high-interest topics** that engage students and build background knowledge in numerous content areas.

■ Articles include **features typical of informational text** such as graphs, charts, maps, and timelines.

■ Articles give students an opportunity to read the kinds of passages typically found on **state tests**.

■ Teacher notes describe ways the articles can be used to **practice *Toolkit* strategies**.

Accompanying **CD-ROMs** provide full-color informational texts in **English** and **Spanish**.

*To learn more or purchase, visit* **Heinemann.com**

Heinemann
DEDICATED TO TEACHERS™

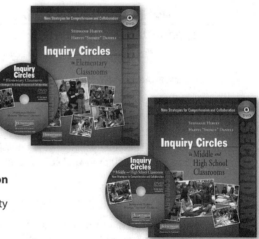